flying Changes

flying Changes

Horses as Spiritual Teachers

Carter Heyward

photographs by Beverly Hall

THE
PILGRIM
PRESS
Cleveland

CARTER, GRETCHEN, AND FREE
REIN STUDENT LINDSEY DUNCAN
ON BUTTERCUP.

In memory of
Sugar and Whisper
and dedicated to
the staff, students, volunteers, and horses at
Free Rein Center for Therapeutic Riding and Education
in Brevard, North Carolina.

All proceeds from this book will go to Free Rein.

The Pilgrim Press, 700 Prospect Avenue, Cleveland, Ohio 44115-1100
thepilgrimpress.com
© 2005 Carter Heyward and Beverly Hall

Printed in the United States of America on acid-free paper

10   09   08   07   06   05   5   4   3   2   1

Library of Congress Cataloging-in-Publication Data
Heyward, Carter.
  Flying changes : horses as spiritual teachers / Carter Heyward ; photographs by Beverly Hall.
    p. cm.
  Includes bibliographical references (p.).
  ISBN 0-8298-1605-4 (pbk. : alk. paper)
  1. Horses—Religious aspects—Christianity. 2. Human-animal relationships. 3. Animals—Religious aspects—Christianity. I. Title.
BT746.H49 2005
248—dc22
                                                                    2004066096

Contents

When a child comes into the world with a talent to transform it, she must be given a chance to work her magic. Otherwise, we are diminished because the world around us and within us has failed again to nurture our possibilities for creativity and beauty.
Could it be that each of us comes into life with a gift that is unique and potentially transformative of our common life? If so, could it be the special mission of a few to help the rest realize what we too can be?

—*Carter Heyward*

Introduction
Remembering Who We Are

"Remember who you are."
—*my sister Ann to her kids*

Angela and I could not find words for it, the sense we had with Red and the other horses. But we knew it had as much to do with God as anything we had encountered, especially in the context of a world teeming as ours is with violence and fear. We knew this because, with the horses, we were tapping roots of courage and strength, hope and amazement. And we knew that these spiritual gifts were preparing us to live more enthusiastically as advocates for a more just and compassionate world.

Learning with Horses

The lessons recorded in this book have been learned with horses. Such lessons and many others are learned by humans all over the world in relation to creature-kind[1]—dolphins and dogs, chimpanzees and cats, rivers and mountains, cows and deserts, birds and stars, flowers and rocks. We can also of course learn much from copperheads and black widows; terrible wind, fire, flood; deer ticks and cockroaches because life is not all harmony, beauty, and peace. We share a world shaped by violence, conflict, and harshness, much of it inherent to our creatureliness, and much of it created or exacerbated by our fear, greed, and self-serving abuses of power, which generate more of the same. Evil sparks evil, just as goodness—that which is compassionate and kind, mutually respectful and generous—gives birth to even greater goodness.

H. Richard Niebuhr, a professor of Christian ethics and theology in the United States in the mid-twentieth century, remarked late in his life that, if he could start again, he would "travel with the poets." He realized that poets often harbor deep perceptions into the heart of things because they don't try to capture them, especially sacred things, with words and bind them in prisons of language. They listen, they watch, they jot down words spaciously and sparsely.

LEVITICUS (LEVI),
YOUNG HORSE BELONGING TO LINDA LEVY,
CARTER'S FRIEND, RIDING INSTRUCTOR,
AND ORIGINAL INSPIRATION FOR THIS BOOK.

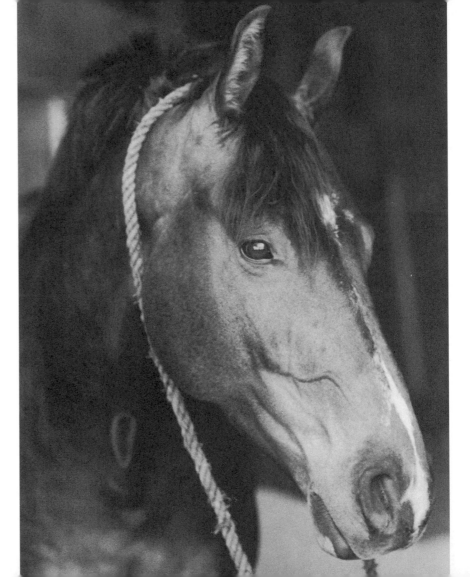

First Impressions

There you are!
but who
or what
are you?
So other than human
flesh you are!

So fast,
sleek, powerful!
You don't just run,

you thunder
on the earth.

We are small
and so very full
of questions!

Can this croning spirit
grow large enough
to meet such a great
other? can I
relax enough
to enjoy you
in my bones
and belly?

Question is:
Can I continue now
content among my own
kind, contained and safe
within boundaries
of what I know
or think I do
about human
and divine
life?

You are so foreign
to us, so other!

How even
to imagine that you
can teach us to live
more fully human
lives?

Question is:
Are we patient
enough
to meet
you

which means learning
to respect you
in your horse-ness
not as a reflection
of our humanness?

Will we live on
fearing so terribly
what we do not
know so well?

Will we live
as strangers,
always
at a distance?

O, we will
live always
at some distance
but perhaps not so much in fear.

Conversion

This book signals a pronounced change in spiritual direction for this Christian liberation theologian—from a more or less human-centered theism to a creation-centered pan-en-theism. From a faith mediated primarily through human-based resources (Jesus, Bible, women, and men) to an awakening to the Sacred in which we live and breathe and die and live, a Power who needs no mediation once we realize that it is She in whom we live.

Looking back, I see that most of what I needed to know about God in the world I knew by the time I was four or five. "Growing up" has been a journey back to that knowledge. Somehow I got it, this creation-centered message. From the Spirit of the indigenous Cherokee peoples who inhabited the land in the U.S. South before my English peoples came and pushed them off, or was it from the land itself, or is this the same Spirit? Very early on I knew that we humans are a small portion of creation, not necessarily the most intelligent, and certainly of no greater spiritual worth than others. I knew this beyond a doubt as a child, but over time this knowledge faded much like a chalk message on an old blackboard that was not quite erased. My education through school, church, and life itself in the mid- to late-twentieth-century United States, though immensely valuable in many ways, has been steeped in ignorance and recklessness in relation to the building of earth community. So steeped that even to speak of "mutuality" with earth and creatures-other-than-human may ring (even in my ears) as mostly fantasy and self-indulgence.

It is indeed imaginative to begin to recognize other animals and earth itself as siblings and parents, friends and lovers. To quote my beloved friend Angela Solling from Australia, "What is imagination if not a window into God, daahling?" (and Angela called everyone "daahling"). It is *phantasie*, theologian Dorothee Soelle's wonderful term for a blending of faith, freedom, and imagination.[2] But mere "fantasy," an escape from reality, it is not; and it is quite the opposite of "self-indulgence," which more nearly describes the motive of much education in the modern and postmodern West.

Troubled by the selfish individualism and materialism of our culture, my parents protested in the best way they knew—by teaching their children some precious counter-cultural lessons, such as the value of placing kindness above all else; the courage to think for ourselves in a world in which few do; and the strength to swim against the popular tide. With these lessons as lifejacket, I decided in my teen years to leap into the currents of progressive religion and, with sister and brother believers, join the movement against racial segregation. This was a turning from which there would be no return, yet other turnings would follow.

Decades later, I speak with a grateful heart. Life as a feminist Christian liberation theologian has been for the most part energizing and exciting, especially as the work has kept me struggling with and among marginalized sisters and brothers: women, queer folk, racial/ethnic/cultural minorities, economically exploited populations, people with special needs and abilities, the earth and its many, varied creatures. I've loved my work, learned more than I could ever have imagined, made true friends, and become ever more radicalized with the passage of time and events in the world right up to the present.

If I could begin again, I wouldn't make many changes. But there is one change I would make, and it is so significant that it surely would have affected everything else in my life, and so all that I am and do, all that I believe and think, would have been different. If I could start over, I would spend more time, serious time and playful time, with the animals. I would take more to heart, as the foundation of intelligence, my strongest intuition as a child to listen to animals and also to plants and rocks. And if I had done this deeper listening, if I had cultivated a super, natural capacity to communicate beyond words with other-than-human-creatures, my life in the world would surely have taken paths that I can barely imagine.

Would I have become a priest? Would I have remained Christian? Perhaps, perhaps not. In any case, I would have been a radical theologian by the time I was about ten and, had I been Christian, I would have realized that the church is profoundly ignorant, spiritually mistaken, in its patronizing disvaluing of the earth and its many varied creatures. This is something I knew as a child, but I didn't grow in this wisdom as I moved through my teen years into adulthood. I didn't sustain or cultivate the deeper knowledge that, as a historical religion, Christianity has been wrong, dead wrong, and way out of touch with reality and what can save us—not the other creatures in and of themselves but all of us, human and others, together struggling for right—mutual—relation. We humans cannot perpetuate the fantasy that we alone are rulers of creation if we hope to survive. I have known this in my bones from the beginning and I have come to know it, gradually and increasingly, as a thinking adult over the last three decades.

This book is about conversion—about turning to the animals for spiritual help. It's a book about the Spirit's involvement with us at depths and in places most Christians, wherever we are in the world, and most Euro-Americans do not recognize because we have not been educated by religion or culture to realize who we are, and who and what we are not. It's about God's efforts to teach us mutuality; about spiritual lessons learned with animals—in this case, horses—companions generally unacknowledged by Christians to be spiritual teachers, because Christian spirituality on the whole has not recognized the vastness and diverse shapes of God's presence and abilities among us in creation, and neither have most Christian theologies over the years and across cultural divides.

Today much creative "eco-theology" is being done around the world by teachers from diverse religious and spiritual traditions, including a number of Christian and post-Christian theologians.[3] This particular book is neither a studied analysis of the spiritual problems inherent to traditional Eurocentric Christianities nor a systematic attempt to construct new theological possibilities, although these pages offer a way of thinking theologically that is meant to draw us more fully into the midst of creation itself as a theological workshop.

Present here are images—some photographs and passages of spiritual prose and theological reflection—meant to evoke recognition of an ancient wisdom, a deeper knowing, that radicalizes spirituality beyond what is normally understood to be "Christian" or for that matter important or even thinkable in the teachings of monotheism. The book invites the reader beyond what most people understand to be "Christian" and, more generally, monotheistic religion. "Monotheism" refers to the religious understanding of a god who is essentially above and beyond humanity and creature-kind, a deity accessible to us only through prophetic voices and saintly visions of such spiritually evolved or divinely appointed persons as the human Jesus. These pages convey no understanding of a god above us; no experience of an all-powerful and all-knowing deity; no belief that there is a god who rules, rewards, and punishes us; most importantly, no assumption that God is more fully involved with humankind than with the rest of creature-kind.

One of the great spiritual travesties, a false and damaging teaching, perpetuated historically by the church against the world's peoples and other creatures is that we humans should think of ourselves as spiritually superior to the rest of creation, closer and more important to God.

The book assumes that God did not, and does not, come to us primarily, much less only, in human form—not simply in Jesus once upon a time and not merely in any of us or our peoples, cultures, and struggles today. Indeed, my faith is in a God that came in Jesus just as God comes all the time in and through our lives, our prayers, and our efforts to build right relation, which is just and compassionate. Right relation, justice, and compassion are the ways of God. This is what the Jesus story is all about—revealing God as the power that forges mutual relation among us, not just humans, but all of us, humans and creatures that are other-than-human, in ways visible and invisible, historical and mystical, close at hand and cosmic.

But the theology in these pages moves beyond simply affirming the sacredness of creation, a theme lifted up by Christian and other spiritual practitioners who see God in earth and sky, animals and plants and rocks. The theology here presupposes that God does not inhere in creation simply to be enjoyed as a source of comfort or dreaded as a dangerous force. God is presented here as a Spirit *actively* moving to touch us and involve us in and through the rest of creation. To be sure, our connectedness with other-than-human creatures is sacred and we do indeed encounter liberating healing power in all creatures great and small. But more even than this, the Spirit of God in all creation is calling us beyond our human- (self-) centered experiences of God *in order to save us*. God is an active life force, not a passive ground upon which we imagine ourselves to live and move as active persons.

Through river and sky, mountain and forest, stone and mud, beloved and abused, respected and ignored, God beckons us to notice the sacred as the struggle for mutual respect. Through sea turtles and brown pelicans, lions and starfish, pileated woodpeckers and black snakes, God pleads with us to recognize holiness as the yearning for right relation: mutuality, not sameness. Mutuality is not simply equality or a leveling of power. Mutuality is the basic dynamic of the universe. It is the energy of our radical interdependence and of our moral responsibility and capacity to realize it and to honor one another in the particularities of who each of us is and what we need to live and thrive if we are to live and thrive together on the earth. Mutuality presupposes our differences, conflicts, and ongoing tensions.

Spiritual Awakening, Theological Transformation, and Social Change

The Sacred Spirit is telling us that the only way we can survive is mutually. Through winter grass and evergreen, garden spider and mountain laurel, white squirrel and speckled hen, she is urging us to realize that our sister and brother creatures embody, as we all do, a knowledge of God that will heal and liberate us—*if we believe*. For indeed only a radical creation faith can save us. This is what our creature kin have to teach us. Their message is that, if we humans hope to be included in the future of the earth, we must find ways of building and sustaining our faith in the sacred power of mutual relation. The Spirit of God beckons us through sea breeze and hail storm: we who have ears, let us hear.

The building of mutuality among humans and between humans and other creatures is the foundation of liberation from all oppression. A vibrant spirituality of creation is a powerful spirituality of liberation. There is no difference. Creation and liberation bubble up from the same wellsprings of mutuality, as it was in the beginning, is now, and will be forever.

This radical presence of a liberating God in all creation is something I have known in my soul since I came bounding into life six decades ago. It is a deep knowledge of God, and it has always been a trustworthy wellspring of my theological intelligence. But this is unnecessarily academic language. The knowledge of God as deeply present in all creatures is potentially a source and resource of every human person's *spiritual* intelligence. Indeed, we who have ears, let us hear, and we who have voices, let us speak.

Over the last ten or fifteen years, this spiritual knowledge has begun to transform how I understand my own vocation as a Christian priest and theologian. It is, I believe, neither arrogant nor an exaggeration to suggest that few Episcopal priests or Christian theologians believe that God is *as* involved in the living and dying of all sea and earth and sky creatures as she was and is in Jesus and you and me. Most Christians, even radical ones, hold to the singularity of Jesus as *the* Son or *the* Christ, a spiritual cut above the rest of us; and most of those who believe that Jesus was, in fact, a brother on the same spiritual plane with others, assume that what Jesus and the rest of us have in common is our *humanness* and, perhaps, our *divinity*, rather than even more basically our creatureliness, which is our embodiedness with all creation, animals, plants, and rocks, and which is also our breath, wetness, hotness, and cold. And we live not only *with* the wind and seas, sun, moon, stars, and ice but also *like* these other partners in creation.

I mean by this that all elements, all species, all communities, all bodies do not just "happen" to be present in the same universe. We are kindred and alike in that the existence of each of us, the fact of our being who and what we are, is connected with all others. Beyond our capacities to know exactly how or how much, we are interdependent creatures. We humans and rocks and trees and birds are "daughters" and "sons" of the same Creator. We belong to the same God; and each of us is as important to God as any other. In this process that we humans call "life," we need one another, and what both human creatures and other creatures need most from human beings is our strong advocacy and the sort of deep respect that acknowledges the presence and worth of others.

This small book reflects a stepping away from both Jesus-centered and human-centered theological assumptions, which I no longer share with most other Christians of whatever politic, identity, or denomination. I offer these reflections because I have come to believe deep in my soul, the root of my spiritual intelligence, that the other creatures are asking to be our spiritual teachers and that learning from them is a source of hope for the world that we share with other humans and with them.

For most of my life—all of it as a theologian—I have worked to present God as our power in the struggle for right, mutual relation rather than as a power over us and I have insisted that we are co-creators with God. As far back as I can remember, I have believed that "we" include not only human beings but all creatures, the whole creation, and that "our power in mutual relation" refers to a Spirit as present in scorpions and snakes, radishes and rocks, as in you and me. I have only begun to make this belief explicit in my theological work since the early 1990s, as my theological passion for social justice has been increasingly rooted in, and informed by, a mystical apprehension of the Spirit in all.

I have always adored dogs and admired pretty much all animals. Like many of my friends, and nearly all of my family members of origin and choice, I have always been an "animal person." I've assumed all along that animals have souls—embodied and animated meeting places of creator and creature. I have never doubted that the rest of creation matters as much to God as we humans do. So it has come as no surprise to me that much of my theological inspiration in recent years has come from animals, most recently horses and the people who love them. What has surprised me has been the extent to which human-horse dynamics have radicalized my experiences of the spiritual landscape, thus also my understandings of who and what God is among us.

Ten years ago, I would have said that God is in horses and elephants and even stones, spiders, and roaches—but that God is with and in human beings in a special way, that we humans are the crown and glory of creation. Increasingly I have come to believe that God is *with* other creatures *as much as* with you and me and that our sister and brother creatures are as deeply glorious to God as we are. Over the past few years, I have begun to see that not only does God's holiness inhere in these spiritual kin of ours. She is trying to reach us through them.

But what does this mean—God actively trying to reach us through other creatures? It means that other creatures, like humans, are infused with a sacred Spirit that is active—stirring, calling, moving through their bodyselves, as she is also moving through humans. It means the God whom Jesus loved is not inactive or silent in trees or stones. It means that we humans share a vocation to learn how to communicate with other creatures, especially how to listen to what is being said to us. That is what the images in these pages are meant to convey—the Spirit's reaching toward us through other creatures in an effort to save us humans from our fear-based, seemingly hell-bent compulsion to destroy the world, ourselves, and other creatures with us.

And what are we to "do" as the Spirit tries to reach us through animals, earth, and other humans? Professional theologians talk a lot about "methodology"—how to "do" theology. This book has a methodology that reflects a way of life that is being proposed through these images and reflections: a way of engaging "otherness," of moving through fear of the "other," a way that requires patience—taking time, waiting, listening, observing—a way of learning, again and again, in each new situation, how to love one another.

Why do I refer to God as "she" and wish to celebrate "her" power, when I am fully and gratefully aware that God transcends the particularities of gender? I am choosing here to signal the transformative power of female/feminine images of sacred power in the context of a world and church that continues to be distorted by patriarchal assumptions not only about gender relations but also war, domination, and the supremacy of humankind over creation. These assumptions, while shared by many women—we are after all patriarchal daughters—are also frequently challenged by women across culture, race, and class. For women in patriarchy, more often than men and usually with greater tenacity, embody resistance not only to male domination but also to the arrogant human assumption that we humans are here to subdue and dominate the earth and its creatures. We can be sure that if most humans experienced God as mother, sister, daughter, lover, and friend, the earth would be a vastly more welcoming home for creatures of all species, including humans. Hence, the image of God in "her" power.

The primary message and method of *Flying Changes* is this: Those who really want to know and honestly come to love other species, other groups of people, or other individuals must learn to be silent, must learn to listen, must learn to observe, must learn to smell and sense and become aware of what we normally miss. We must learn to wait quietly and patiently if we are to discover again, in each new time and space, how to communicate, how to speak, how to touch, how to love, and how to be loved by others—especially those who are different from us in ways *that are significant to us or them*, on the basis of race, culture, religion, sexuality/gender, age, ability, or species.

Creature-kind and Our Salvation

Obviously, I do not believe that God "prefers" humans to snails or, for that matter, horses to jellyfish. Still, whether or not there is some "order" of significance in the universe is something we had best leave to God, whose mysterious ways of weaving us together in and beyond the world as we know it have not been revealed to us. Most Christians, including this one, believe that at some place beyond this world and some time beyond time as we measure it we will "see" more clearly what we now see "through a glass dimly." It may well be that the lilies of the field are even closer to the heart of the Sacred, the

CARTER HEYWARD AND MACHO,
A 20-YEAR-OLD PASO FINO GELDING
(NEUTERED MALE) WHO WAS A GIFT
FROM A NEIGHBOR.
MACHO HAS BECOME ONE OF
FREE REIN CENTER'S FAVORITE
THERAPY HORSES AND IS MUCH BELOVED BY
CHILDREN AND ADULTS FOR HIS UNUSUALLY
SWEET SPIRIT AND SMOOTH GAITS. MACHO IS
ALSO THE MOST MELLOW OF THE HORSES WHO
HAVE BECOME CARTER'S
COMPANIONS OVER
THE LAST FIVE YEARS.

core of holiness, than we humans can be, given all of our moral confusion. But we don't know about this and we won't for awhile yet. In the meantime, Christian and other ethicists will, and should, continue to debate the extent to which animal well-being should, or should not, be compromised on behalf of human health and, far too often, human greed and whim. My advocacy of animal well-being and environmental justice grows slowly stronger in uneven rhythm the longer I pray and struggle with such questions.

I cannot deny what I am hearing. Against the terrible backdrop of war and rumors of war, the Spirit is yearning, as ever, be born among us, urging us toward opening more fully to her presence and her needs. No stranger to fear and terror, conflict and tension, violence and killing, she nonetheless generates peace, always peace. She also brings death as well as life, fear as well as comfort. The animals and other creature-kind are key to our salvation for they can help us see that we Christians seldom encourage one another to experience fear and even death, not as evil or as punishment, but rather as sometimes terrible dimensions of life in the realm of the Spirit. To be sure, our fear of difference, otherness, and unknownness can, and often does, function demonically in our lives, leading us into evil. In these cases, death too often is a consequence of injustice, oppression, evil. But neither fear as an emotion, nor death as a passage beyond life as we know it, is in itself ungodly. The rest of creature-kind embody fear and death, these dimensions of our shared life in God, in ways that can help us realize that through fear and someday death, we may come face to face with the Sacred in her great wisdom. Meanwhile, we simply do not, and cannot, fathom the mystery of God.

Sisters in the Saddle

This book reflects God's awakening in me through my relationship with horses and people who know and love them—especially Linda Levy, a remarkable horse trainer and riding instructor in suburban Boston, and several friends who have been working with us: my beloved companion Sister Angela (who died early in 2002), and Angela's and my friends Gretchen Grimshaw and Beverly Hall, both horse lovers, mystical Christians, seminarians (when I first met them), and women who share a passion for a more just and compassionate world. Linda Levy has been a mentor to Angela, Gretchen, and me for several years, teaching us what horses teach her and helping us become more attuned to what they can teach us. Our friend Beverly Hall has become a partner in this writing and photography project, helping us more fully "image" the spirituality and theology we have been learning with Linda.

Working with Linda has done more than make us better riders. The lessons with Linda deepened Sister Angela's mystical apprehension of the light of God in all creation. Similarly, these lessons have sharpened my awareness of God and radicalized my faith as a Christian mystic and social activist, simply because the more deeply engaged I have become with horses and the people who love them, the more astonishing my awareness that we are all connected. As a sister in Sacred Spirit, I share with all sisters and brothers a moral obligation to struggle toward a more just and compassionate world for all of us, humans and others. Gretchen Grimshaw has begun working with Linda more recently and is also being drawn by the Spirit beyond simply learning to ride her horses Patience and Izzy. Like Angela and me, Gretchen is being nudged by the Spirit to accept some special gifts being offered to us through creation in general and, at this time, horses in particular. For Gretchen, too, Linda Levy has been a significant mentor.

Though infused with Linda, Angela, Gretchen, and Beverly Hall's friendships and insights, *Flying Changes* for the most part reflects my particular experiences of God, as well as Beverly Hall's and my efforts to communicate images of these experiences to you, the reader. Linda's responses to my experiences of her as a *spiritual* mentor have ranged from mild surprise—since Linda's intention is to teach horseback riding, not theology—to appreciative affirmation because she also recognizes the spirituality in the horse-human connection. The reader should understand, however, that this book's theology should be interpreted as mine, not Linda Levy's, Gretchen Grimshaw's, or photographer Beverly Hall's. Some of my theological assumptions these women share, some they don't, and even those they do would be communicated differently were Linda or Gretchen writing this book or were Beverly Hall on her own organizing and presenting these lessons through her photography.

Sister Angela and I actually discussed endlessly, it seemed, and explored with shared enthusiasm much of the content in these pages as the spirituality reflected here was taking shape between us over a three-year period. So this book is, in many ways, Angela's as much as it is mine, though it may be unfair of me to make this claim since Angela has "jumped the twig" and can no longer look at me across the breakfast table and say, "daahling, I don't agree with this!"

Still, I am confident that Angela would join me in affirming that the web of women and horses contributing to the authorship of *Flying Changes* suggests that we humans can share life-giving, mutually empowering experiences—relating to horses, children, food, music, whatever—without having to agree on their spiritual meanings or religious significance, even though sometimes we do agree, profoundly. In other words, we can (in my language) "god" together without necessarily agreeing on who or what God is or even if God is at all—and still be living, struggling, working, and playing together in the world of God.

Healing and Liberation: Some Retrospective Spiritual Musings

Growing up in the mountains of Carolina, I knew that whatever God was, he or she or it was very much larger than all the pictures and portrayals of God in the Christian Bible. How did I "know" this? I knew by the squishy feel of God between my toes in the wet grass and the dramatic crashing and splashing of God as waterfall. I knew that God was calling us beyond the huge and ugly divide between "white" and "colored" people and that God was somehow "in" our best dreams of a world in which every creature is cherished, not just humans like us or different from us.

The God who met me in people was as "colored" as she was "white." Truth be known, she was more "colored" than "white" because it was clear to the six-year-old me that God enjoyed a special place among the poor, and the poor among us were so often, it seemed to me, "colored." And this same God of poor folks and all folks who welcomed her was a Spirit that barked and ran on four feet and rolled around on the ground with me.

I could taste God in the juice of apples that fell from trees in the yard and I believed that God was entirely present in the communion services my friends and I conducted from time to time with coconut meat and milk. It was clear to me that we were priests, my friends and I—young priests of a God who calls all children and creatures, even adults, into radically mutual relation with one another and God.

Now this is more or less what I've been teaching in my work as a seminary professor and Episcopal priest for three decades. It is what I, one lesbian feminist Christian theologian, have believed—that God is our power in mutual relation and that Jesus, a brother, showed us how "to god."

No fool, however, I have realized from at least my early teen years that this vast, inclusive experience of a Spirit urging us ever more fully into mutuality runs counter to what the church, state, and larger society teach us about God, ourselves, and what is best in the world. And so I have known for decades that, if we wish to live in this Spirit of radical mutuality, we can expect to struggle against the forces that control the world and its various institutions, including the church. These forces control not only the vast external structures and systems of our lives, but also our psyches, spiritualities, and what we tend to think of as our "personal" or "private" lives. Indeed, our inner lives to various degrees are shaped and sustained through our attachments to seductive spirits of domination and submission, deities of consumerism, militarism, nationalism, patriotism, other gods that promise, if we bow down to them, to protect us.

Thanks to wise parents, good friends, and mentoring from several wonderful teachers in church, school, and college, I knew that much of what passed for "normalcy" and "the good life" among white middle-class Christians in the United States in the 1950s and 1960s was, at best, pleasant and enjoyable, like a great vacation at the beach or a homemade lemon pound cake. But I didn't enter young adulthood in the late 1960s under any illusion that the prevailing systems of value and allegiance, in either church or nation, had much to do with God. Not the God whom Jesus had loved, the Spirit urging us to join in co-creating a world in which justice and peace kiss each other.

What I could not have realized as an enthusiastic teen or even as a younger adult with a passion for justice was that, over time, we are bound to be worn down by those social, religious, political, and psychological forces that want no part of what we represent or who we are. One of the ways some, probably many, folks cope with this kind of social wear and tear and personal exhaustion is through addictions of various forms. For me, an addiction to alcohol served for many years to numb the pain of the struggle. In 1985, I sought help and stopped drinking. Once I didn't have the substance to fall back on, I became aware of how tired I had become. For the first time in my life—I was forty years old—I not only was exhausted in the marrow of my bones; I *felt* the exhaustion and wondered how I could go on.

The next couple of decades, up to the present time, have been for me a period of healing, and not simply on a personal level. Life in the world has been teaching me how radically social and political our so-called "personal" journeys are. We ignore our collectivity and social histories as people of different cultures, races, gender identities, classes, religions, and other variables at our peril. The terror attacks of September 11, 2001, exemplified the extent to which we are *collectively* in harm's way in no small part because we Christians in the United States have turned our backs on the needs of most of the world's peoples and other creatures to be accorded dignity, respect, and common decency. As my friend Muriel Kinsey has observed, "It's what we turn our backs on that finally comes and stares us down."[4] This is what is happening to the United States today and also to Christians and people of diverse faith traditions who have ignored the urgent cry of humans and other creatures around the world. These brothers and sisters have come to stare us down.

Going South, Going North

Since the mid-1980s and the early days of my recovering from alcoholism, I had been wanting, and needing, to move away from full-time seminary teaching in order to nourish my spiritual and political energies and strengthen my work as a teacher, theologian, priest, and activist. In 1998, with my life-companions, I moved back to the mountains of North Carolina, where I have spent half of each year. The other half of the year I have continued to teach theology in Massachusetts.

Wonderfully and quite unexpectedly, an old mare named Sugar arrived in my life in the summer of 1999. With her arrival began the spiritual transformation reflected in this book. I should say the transformation *continued*, because it actually had begun several years earlier, in 1991, when I met Sister Angela, a Franciscan nun, mystic, priest, and renowned sculptor in Australia who would become my soul mate and a beloved friend and life-companion. Shortly before Christmas 1999 and several months after Sugar had arrived in my life, Sister Angela joined our small intentional community in the mountains of western North Carolina.

Each January Angela and I would return to Massachusetts, where I teach the spring semester at the Episcopal Divinity School and where, until her death in 2002, Angela worked as artist-in-residence in an Episcopal parish. For the two spring seasons we were together in Massachusetts, Angela and I took riding lessons from Linda Levy. We were trying to become more than simply good riders; we wanted to be better horsewomen, learning how to meet horses in a spirit of mutuality, which we believed to be the Spirit of God. The rest of each year—summer, fall, and early winter—Angela and I lived in North Carolina, where we volunteered at Free Rein Center for Therapeutic Horseback Riding, an organization we had helped found in 2000.

Linda Levy: Equestrian, Mentor

"We always knew she had some special mission in life, which is why we named her 'Linda,' which means 'God's blessing.'"
—Joan and Robert Day, Linda Levy's parents

"I think my mother is a horse!"
—Hannah Lavin, Linda Levy's daughter

I met Linda Levy in the winter of 2000 when I arrived for my lesson at a riding stable near Boston. Having been interviewed by phone and assigned to a nice gentle school horse, I led my pony, Mary Lou, into the arena, mounted, and sat there waiting to meet the teacher. Someone had pointed her out to me: Linda—a short, round woman, bundled in a winter jacket, braid sticking out of a winter cap. At first glance she was not readily identifiable as one of the best riding teachers and horse trainers anyone who knows her and knows horses has ever met. Over the next few years, I would begin to understand the mentoring power of this woman. Linda is connected with horses deep in her soul and, clearly, in theirs as well. This soulful connection between woman and horse empowers her to relate respectfully to horses. And her respect of the horse evokes the horse's respect of her, a mutuality that fosters communication.

Across time Angela, Gretchen, and I would discover that Linda is more than simply a good horseback riding instructor. She would likely be called a "horse whisperer" by many horse people, but she distances herself from the term, which she views as a contemporary rip-off and trivialization of an ancient ability. Among horses and people who love them, Linda Levy is a healer of broken spirits and an inspiration to live more fully into what feminist theologian Nelle Morton named our power "to hear one another to speech."[5] Linda knows and teaches that this is what horses can do if we learn to listen to them. They can hear us to speech, helping empower us to live in our strength.

The lessons with Linda have been basically about horses and horseback riding. For Linda, the equestrian, that's what it's all about. For me the lessons have also been about the sacredness between us, the power we meet "in the relation" between and among us rather than simply inside any one of us, human or horse. Not that we cannot find God "in" ourselves, but the God we find within is the Spirit between us, a sacred power who gives birth again and again, always in the relation between and among the creatures, people and stars, plants and animals, stones and the one who creates us. Just as she presents herself and is born again in each moment in which two or more of us are gathered together, so too is she born again each time a person, a horse, or perhaps even a blade of grass, in some way "remembers" another one.

But even to use a word like "remember" in this context suggests a difficulty we humans have imagining, much less experiencing or communicating through words, how creatures other than human are involved with us in the spiritual processes of brokenness and healing, oppression and liberation. Language can be as much a barrier to our experiences of God as a creative spiritual resource. Words impede communication as often as they enable it. This is true among people and it is even more the case between us and other creatures. We can talk "at" horses until we're blue in the face and we will get little response. Learning to communicate with horses, really to listen and really to hear, is a different matter. It's about remembering who we are together and communicating. Not necessarily talking.

One day, early in my lessons with Linda Levy, I was having a hard time on the horse I had leased for the spring of 2000. "You've got to communicate with your horse, Carter!" Linda said as the horse Mary Lou and I trotted by. Well-schooled in an academic culture that equates communication with verbal exchange, I began talking to Mary Lou. A moment later, I heard Linda shouting at me from the far side of the arena, "Carter, I said 'communicate,' not 'talk'! *Communicate* with Mary Lou!"

Linda did not mean that talking to the horse isn't sometimes an important part of communication but rather that there is so much more to our engagement with one another—human to horse, human to human, creature to creature—than using words, so much more to communication than talking, so much more to language than words.

Remembering Who We Are

The lessons I want to share in this book are about communicating as a process of re-membering who we are together: putting back together what has been dismembered in our lives and world, our histories and cultures, our consciousnesses and cosmos. What has been dismembered, torn apart, shattered has been our mutual sense of connectedness with one another, including other than human creatures. The Spirit urges us to remember who we are. Remembering, we return not to a primordial paradise but literally to our senses. As our senses sharpen and we become better able to *feel*, we are better able to think more honestly, which in turn seasons our intelligence. The more spiritually intelligent we become, the better able we are to wrestle creatively with good and evil—and to recognize evil when we see it: violence and domination, cruelty and exploitation, greed and apathy.

In these pages, the Spirit meets us primarily through the human-horse relation. It is not that horses have more to teach us than, say, cats or dogs, birds or gerbils, caterpillars or trees, rocks or water. Why then horses? Why not image the healing power of dogs, for example—especially since many more of us today have canine companions than horses and since I, for one, have known dogs longer and much more intimately than I know horses?

The book focuses on horses, not because I am an expert horsewoman, which I am not, but because horses are, for me, particularly compelling spiritual teachers. The spiritual awakening that horses can offer their human companions is rooted in particular experiences of struggling for balance, coping with fear, and patiently taking time for what matters—experiences shared by horses and humans. Other lessons conveyed in these pages could as easily spring forth from our relationships with many other species of creatures—lessons about passion, otherness, beauty, and whimsy or lightness of being.

May these lessons draw the reader more consciously into the realm of Spirit to perceive more clearly who we are—we creatures of many species, we humans of many kinds, in a world and time we share.

Beverly Hall is working in these pages as a photojournalist, trying to help us—me, the author, you, the reader—*see* what is going on as horses and humans struggle for mutuality. Through her photographs and my use of language, Beverly and I are recording what I, along with Angela and Gretchen, have been learning about horses, especially from Linda Levy. More than any other human represented in these pages, Linda is passing on a spiritual intelligence, a wisdom, that can enable riders and horses to find a balanced way of relating, to experience and work through fear together, to take the time we need to foster mutuality, and even to make "flying changes"—to be able to dance together as we turn—horse and human together. As an equestrian feat, a flying change is a graceful, energetic movement that demonstrates considerable skill on the part of both horse and rider. As a spiritual metaphor, it signals conversion, a "turning." It is as a theological writer who loves horses, not an accomplished equestrian, that I pass on what I am learning because it is revolutionizing my experiences of the Sacred.

HANNAH LAVIN, LINDA'S DAUGHTER,
DOING A "FLYING CHANGE" WITH GUINNESS.

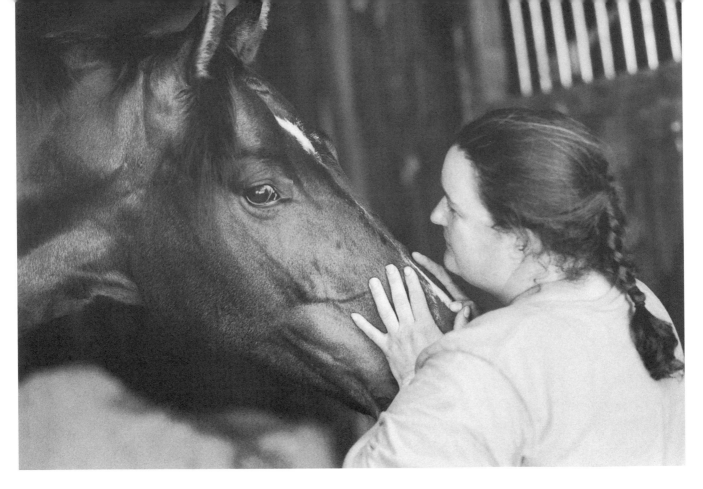

LINDA AND LEVI. THE YEARNING FOR PASSIONATE CONNECTION MAY BE OUR MOST DEEPLY MORAL DESIRE
BECAUSE IT INFUSES US WITH SACRED POWER.

One *Passion*
Being Really Present

Most of us don't realize how absent we often are in our love and work: absent, apathetic, passionless. We spend much of our lives missing one another, which means we are missing our lives.

A Special Mission

Linda Day was born with a passion for horses, but she didn't begin to know them until a Vermont farmer invited her to come see the horses at his dairy farm several miles down the road from where Joan and Robert Day lived with their six children. Linda was ten at the time and the youngest. From as far back as anyone can remember, Linda had been wild about horses. "They were absolutely central," she recalls. "I didn't even learn to read until I was nine and started reading horse books." Her mother concurs, "Linda didn't show interest in school or reading or much of anything unless it had to do with horses."

Joan Day was a homemaker and Robert Day taught mechanical engineering at a local college. With their five older children, two daughters followed by triplets, the Days were lucky to make ends meet. Prior to Linda's birth they had become Christians and they remember praying before the arrival of their last child. Joan Day reflects thoughtfully, "You know, we had a very special feeling about this child. We knew she had a mission of some sort. We didn't know what. But we knew she was special, which is why we named her 'Linda,' which means 'God's blessing.'" It didn't occur to these gentle people that this child's "special mission" would carry her across species lines and that, before she reached adulthood, their youngest child would learn more about love, respect, and communication from horses than many humans learn from other people.

They did know very early in her life that Linda wanted a horse. As much as they wanted her to have a horse or at least horseback riding lessons, the Days couldn't afford it. "My dad was a school teacher, and there was no way," Linda states as a matter of fact. "I just accepted it. That was the reality."

The English (and Euro-American) culture of competitive riding, of show horses and sports horses like racers and jumpers, is pricey. Then and now, most folks don't enter it without money, and lots of it, because there's no way to stay with horseback riding and horse care without money, not if you're interested in competition and achievement. First come lessons, boots, and helmets; then come shows and fancier dress. Sooner or later, a youngster who is seriously into riding wants her own horse; then comes board and tack; vet and farrier expenses; more lessons, more shows, more clothes. Over time another horse, better suited to the accomplished young rider, may come; followed by a trailer and a truck to pull it, more travel expenses, and equipment, and on it goes. Which is why, in the United States, the world of English show and sports riding at the top levels of competition has long belonged to the upper classes.

Linda Day's early life was shaped in the tension between craving a connection with horses and being a child of middle-class parents who honestly didn't know how to encourage her to pursue such a dream. This tug between the economic class location, which the Days had in common with most people, and the privileged world of fancy horses remained a major force in Linda's life as she grew into her professional stature.

Decades later, a similar pull between the arenas of equine competition at high levels and her commitment to the well-being of both horses and humans stirred in Linda some important questions about personal values, priorities, and financial security. These questions propelled her, through an early marriage and several bouts of depression, more fully toward maturity as a horsewoman and toward health as a human being. In her twenties and thirties, she struggled to cast her lot with the horses and the people who love them against the strong currents of economic exploitation and psychological pressure that dominate the most competitive English show arenas and racetracks, as well as the daily lives of most people in the United States.

Linda's personal and significant professional struggle for the well-being of horses and humans has deep roots in her early passion, a healthy obsession with horses, a steely determination that would not be subdued by the economic realities of middle- and working-class America.

Twisted Passion, Apathy, and Real Presence

Most of us are both drawn to and terrified of such passion. We are moved by the passion that meets us in stories like Linda's, but we are also frightened not only of the suffering that passion often involves but also the intensity of living passionately. To live passionately is to linger in the depths of our shared creaturely and human experience. It is a way of remembering who we are that reflects the image of God, the depths and heights of divine life. Passionate people yearn for mutual relation and this yearning for mutuality is a yearning for God.

Twisted Passion

Yet we live in a world broken by dynamics of violence, through which our passion can, and often does, get twisted. Sexual abuse is a primary example of human passion—our sacred yearning for mutuality, our deep hunger for God, a powerfully erotic power—having been distorted by dynamics of domination and violence, by which humans learn deep in our embodied selves to experience domination and subordination, objectifying others and being objectified, as pleasurable. The sexual abuse crisis in the Roman Catholic Church (in truth, a crisis throughout the churches, to varying degrees) and the tragedy of priests like John Geoghan is at root a crisis of distorted passion. Goeghan's hunger for God was distorted by a compulsive, embodied experience of God's power as the power to objectify and dominate and/or to be objectified and dominated. The far greater problem—which the church cannot acknowledge and still continue to hold fast to its patriarchal moorings—is the extent to which a theology of domination and submission, control and obedience, has been theologically codified as the essence of a patriarchal God's passion. Historically, Roman Catholic and Protestant churches have insisted that domination and submission is how God relates to his creatures, including his Son Jesus on the cross. This theology codifies violence, incliding sexual abuse, as intrinsic to "Christian life."

Linda's affirmation of the life-giving character of passion flies in the face of the dominant Christian culture's association of passion with its distortions: sexual abuse, violence, suffering, and death. In such a dreadful context, the girl child with a passion for horses represents every boy and girl longing to connect with whatever moves against such violence and abuse and generates, instead, an energy for life, healing, and liberation.

Another decadent twist of human passion is evident in how most of us treat animals. Most people in this society can barely conceive of the possibility of building mutuality with each other, much less with creature-kind. It sounds so flaky and idealistic as to be hollow. To most of us, at least in the so-called developed world, an animal is an "it"—never a "thou."[1] For a girl child like Linda Day to take an interest in the actual well-being of animals and creature-kind was to step through an opening into the passion of God. With good friends and wise mentoring, such a child may realize that, even though she, like all of us, is a child of patriarchy, she is also a sister of Spirit yearning passionately for the Sacred, which she can experience through mutual relation, with horses, or dogs, or birds, or trees—and, if she is lucky, with some humans as well.

APATHY

Hate is closer than apathy to love. This is true because apathy is passionless. As an aversion to suffering, apathy is disengagement from the depths and heights of human and divine life, creaturely and creative yearning. We choose to feel little and do nothing rather than risk being hurt. By contrast, when we hate, we are connected emotionally and energetically with those whom we hate; and wherever there is any connection, there is always the possibility of transformation. Through the power of forgiveness—our forgiveness of those who have harmed us and others' forgiveness of us when we ourselves have caused hurt and damage to them—the Sacred can begin to weave strands of hatred into new garments. Our apathy, however, functions as a shield against God as well as the world. And, although personal change and social transformation are always possible, it's a harder stretch—even, we can imagine, for God—to reach apathetic people and begin to wake us up and stir our passion.

Today the Spirit is yearning for apathetic people to wake up from our spiritual slumber and join humanity and creation in a resurrected passion for justice-love, compassion, and nonviolent resistance to evil.

REAL PRESENCE

What then does this Spirit require of us? Horses can help us answer this question because horses, like God, require of us a particular quality of presence. Any horse whom we hope to really know and love requires passionate presence—honest presence, not pretense; full presence, not half-hearted attendance. Those who come half-heartedly, indifferently, or absent-mindedly to horses will not be comfortable with the horses. They will sense rightly that they are in harm's way.

Those who bring themselves more fully to horses will be increasingly concerned about the horses' well-being and are likely to want to know more about horses in general and especially about the particular horse or horses whom they are getting to know. They will also begin to experience themselves in new ways. Girl after girl and woman after woman has told me how, once she began to know a horse, her life began to change. My friend Peg says, "Topper has given me a new confidence!" A Free Rein student exclaims, "I tell Macho everything!" A fellow student in my riding class attests, "I never knew how much of my life I would want to give to anything until Max came along." One young woman at our stables in North Carolina said, "Being around the stables has helped me think of someone other than myself."

When I see how the girls and women and a few boys and men are connecting with horses, I sense that the Spirit is working through the horses to get our attention. Could it be that, through interactions with horses, folks who care about them are being drawn close to a God who is indeed an infinitely abundant wellspring of love and compassion, generosity and mutuality, a Spirit urging us to risk being more fully present in the world wherever we are and with whomever?

Whisper and the Struggle for Justice-love[2]

If horses or any other creatures were genuinely respected by humans as the God-bearers they are, we would all know more about creature-kind, including how to listen to other creatures. Native Americans are among the few tribes of humanity anywhere on this planet who historically have respected horses for who and what they are in themselves and not merely for what they can do, or be, for humans. It's not that we shouldn't ride them, not even that we shouldn't show them or race them playfully and competitively. Horses are big, strong animals. Many horses seem to enjoy racing, jumping, showing off, having a grand old time running around with each other and with their people. The problem that humans have created for horses is the same one we've created for the whole human and other-than-human creation: In our greed, our fear, and our willingness to use violence to solve our conflicts, we humans have created equine cultures of oppression and violence in which we use and abuse horses, simply as we please.

In our stables in the mountains of western North Carolina we have several horses who were treated badly by previous owners. "Whisper" was rescued by a friend from a man who was starving her. By the time she was liberated from this abusive man, Whisper was skin and bones and had lost most of her teeth attempting to eat dirt and stones. Because you tell a horse's age by looking at her teeth, we have no idea how old Whisper is. We do know that, as she slowly gains weight, muscles, strength, her eyes are reflecting less despair, though people continue to comment on Whisper's "sad eyes." To me, Whisper's eyes reflect the pathos of God—a divine sadness—about the state of affairs we humans have created on planet earth. Whisper is a creature whose body bears witness to the twisted shape of our human apathy. Her presence reminds me that to be immersed in God's passion is to love God's body—in this case, the body of a horse who represents to me all creatures and creation itself. Whisper's body is infused with Spirit, luring me to seek right relation with all creatures and to do whatever possible on behalf of a world, a nation, and a society in which all creatures, humans and others, are respected and well cared for.

How can anyone who cares about creation be indifferent to the political situation? As a Christian, I am appalled that we who claim to love Jesus can let ourselves be lulled into an apathy that puts people in positions of political power who don't care much, if at all, about the survival, dignity, and well-being of creatures, human or other. Why do we allow such transparently greedy and fearful men (and some women too) to rise, again and again, to power and turn their backs on the rest of humanity and all creatures except their wealthy cronies?

People who love creation need to be alert to how hostile the policies of the government of the United States are toward the earth and creature-kind, including most humans. If we care about the earth and its many, varied creatures including ourselves, we need to realize that our federal government is becoming increasingly contemptuous toward environmental protections and ecological concerns, as well as toward the social struggles for racial, gender, sexual, economic, and other forms of justice. This contempt undergirds the selfish use and abuse of human and other creatures. Simply by her presence in my life, Whisper urges me to stay with the struggle for a saner world and a more just and compassionate nation.

Meeting One Another

My horse Red was also treated badly in her early days. She manifests several traits that suggest she's known some abuse, though nowhere nearly as much as Whisper. When Red arrived in my life in June 2000 as a fourteen-year-old mare, she was head-shy—no one could touch her face; she also had some difficulty paying attention to people. One of her great features, however—though frightening to me at first—is her strong personality. She's a willful horse who wants to do her own thing and who seems, even more than most horses, to keep her own counsel, which is a very "horsey" quality.

I have had to learn how to listen to Red, how to "read" her, how to communicate with her. It has become clear to me over time that I have to meet Red where she is if I expect her to meet me where I am. But what does this mean—to meet a horse where she is?

When we come into the presence of anyone, how do we tell "where they are" and get a sense of how we might "meet" them in a spirit of respect?

First, we slow down. Take time. We begin to sense whatever we can by looking, listening, smelling.

We may or may not speak. We may stay silent.

We may decide to wait for the other to take notice of us, acknowledge us, make a move in our direction, before we speak or reach out to touch or do anything at all.

In most of our interactions with other people, our "meetings" usually happen so fast that we are on "automatic." We seldom pay attention to where we or others "are" in the here and now or to where we may be headed relationally. Often, in our meetings with strangers, we are inclined either to rush in or hold back. In the former case, we are oblivious to where the other is. In the latter, we are protecting ourselves from the other. In relation to horses, neither of these modes of meeting will do. Horses require an openness to who they really are. We cannot meet them either by rushing in or by holding back.

Red requires that I take lots of time with her. Trying to hurry her or our relationship produces only frustration for us both. On the other hand, to the extent that, in my fear of her, I hold myself back from Red, she turns her back on me as if to say, "See if I care." Slowly I've come to realize that the only way for me to meet Red respectfully is by insisting that she meet me respectfully in the space we are creating between us. This has meant standing up to Red, not letting her ignore me, much less snap at me or threaten to push me over. At the same time, I have spent hours standing with Red, observing her, talking softly to her, sometimes simply standing beside her with a hand on her back or neck. Red often turns away from me when I ask for her attention. I am learning how to hang in with her and wait for her to come around, which she usually does.

Slowly, ever so slowly, over many months, and with Linda's help, I've been able to experience Red as increasingly willing to meet me where I am—someone who loves her and wants to know her and who is still new to the world of horses. I can tell that Red has learned that she must be patient with me and that I really am trying to connect with her and stand with her.

Life with Red has become an ongoing negotiation between human and horse, Carter and Red, back and forth, her way, my way, try this, try that. After four years together, she and I are still in what seems to me to be our early days of learning how to move together gracefully through our fears and frustrations.

Yearning to Know Our Place

Through relationship with Red, Whisper, and my first horse Sugar, I have begun to sense that we are being called by our ancestors—spirits of humans, horses, and other creatures that know us better than we know ourselves—to listen to one another. These spirits yearn to draw us passionately more fully into God and shape us as better lovers of one another, the world, the creatures, and God. Through my relationship with the horses, I have come to believe that these same wise spirits invite animals like Red, Sugar, and Whisper to join up with those who respect and listen to them as we journey together more fully into the life of the liberating One. Thanks to the horses, I have come to believe that, in the rush and clamor of the world around and within us, the yearning for authentic—passionate—connection may be our most deeply moral desire because it literally infuses us with God. Maybe it also makes us more like other creatures, more deeply rooted in the experiences of creature-kind, more fully involved with the Spirit between us, more soulful.

Passion can be after all another word for soul. And whatever on earth, besides bad religious teaching, has led us to imagine that we humans are the only creatures that yearn for passionate, mutual friendship and connection with others? Why do we suppose that we are the only creatures who hunger for God? How did we fall into this terrible sin of pride and arrogance, placing ourselves at the center of all value and goodness? It is this sin that alienates us not only from the rest of creation but also from other humans and our own best selves.

In the fifth century C.E., St. Augustine and with him the Christian church came to believe that our deepest ("original") sin was concupiscence, by which Augustine meant sexual lust or sexual passion. What Augustine failed to see—or, if he saw, failed to clarify—was that the problem with concupiscence, or lust, is not sexual feelings or sexual activity, which can be mighty channels of God's love and God's power. The problem with unbridled lust, as also with greed, violence, and other sources of evil in the world is that they are steeped in our putting ourselves at the center. Our "sin" should not be understood as primarily, if at all, about sex but rather about putting ourselves at the center of everything, the center of God and the world and everything that was, is, or will be—and then making "God" in our image. Worshipping "God" only because "he" is like those of us with the social power to put ourselves at the center and then to define and name "God." It is the sin of "not knowing our place,"[3] the sin of imagining that our ways of being are more sanctified and our lives closer to God than those of other humans and other species. In fact, all violence, oppression, and evil—including sexual violence and abuse—are steeped in this sin of arrogant self-centeredness and self-absorption.

Mystical Possibilities

Mystics are immersed in the passion of God. They can accompany us spiritually beyond words because they are able to meet God in touch, smell, sight, sounds of various sorts, and no sound at all. Sister Angela was a mystic, surely the most explicit, buoyant, and enthusiastic mystic at the stables in both Massachusetts and North Carolina, but Angela would be the first to insist that a mystic is, at heart, the girl who prays while mucking out a stall, the boy who meets God in the body of a horse, the woman who experiences time in slow motion while riding, the man who listens to horses. We are a mystical bunch, we folks at the stables, because we assume that God is as much in, with, and through the horses as with us. We know that, for our relationships with horses—and God—to be right and mutual, we have to learn how to listen to horses, as we do also to God. For most of us, the call to listen to horses and know what they are telling us, their requirement that we meet them where they are, is a real challenge, because horses are so different from us, so "other" than who we are. Most of us do not know the language of horses. If we want to communicate with them, we must learn their "language" just as we expect them to learn ours. Passion is, after all, real presence, the stuff of mutuality, whether the "others" in our lives are horses, trees, or humans.

CARTER AND SUGAR.
SUGAR HAS TAUGHT ME SO MUCH ABOUT OTHERNESS.
AS I GOT TO KNOW HER, I REALIZED THAT SHE WAS UNLIKE
ANYTHING OR ANYONE I'D KNOWN BEFORE.
PERHAPS THE SAME WAS TRUE FOR HER?

Two *Otherness*
Remembering What We *Aren't*

Our salvation as people and as a planet is in learning to love, respect, and cherish others in their "otherness." Respecting an "other" involves becoming aware of the unique personality, spirit, and culture of the particular other, be it a group, a person, a creature, a species. The Sacred who encounters us through horses urges us to notice her also in other people and cultures, other creatures and species, other languages and images of Spirit with which we are neither at home nor necessarily at ease. Only in this way can we begin to create any genuinely mutual relation.

The Spirit between Us

We experience God within us, and this same God is even more fully and completely the Spirit between us, and not just "us" and those "like" us but the Spirit between and among us all, in our variety and differences, however "other" or "alien" we may seem from one another. God connects us and thrives in our interdependencies, carrying us on and re-forming us from one generation to another, one culture to another, one species to another. God is constantly being born amidst our differences. We literally cannot "god"—live holy lives, generating mutuality—without one another.

We may think we are independent and that we don't really need other people or species in order to be ourselves. But this is a big lie, a spiritual delusion crafted out of our big sin of human arrogance. Just as a little child can lead a whole people toward liberation, so too can the pelicans, the whales, the horses help make us free. If we can meet them in their otherness and let them meet us in ours, we can together weave the mutuality that is at the heart of the Sacred.

Linda and Synomi—Encountering Otherness

To help finance the raising and training of standard-bred racehorses, a business she and her first husband Michael began in 1983, Linda, then in her early twenties, sold her own riding horses. For the next several years her energies went into helping their racehorse business take off.

Even more importantly to Linda, her energies were poured into the birth in 1985 of her daughter, Hannah, and the early years of mothering. By the time Hannah was two or three and the racehorse business was five or six, Linda realized she wanted—truth be known, she needed—a riding horse for herself, a nice athletic type, a jumper whom she could enjoy. She heard that someone was selling a former racehorse, a seven-year-old thoroughbred mare, for a thousand bucks.

"Beautiful!" Linda thought when she saw Synomi. Normally, she would have tested a horse before purchase, taking at least one ride to make sure the match was right. But this moment wasn't quite normal for Linda. Something about this particular horse compelled her to buy Synomi there on the spot and take her home.

She was eager to ride this stunningly athletic-looking horse. Already an experienced horsewoman, Linda knew to longe her first. ("Longeing" is a form of ground work, in which a trainer gets the horse to move in small circles around the trainer. It's a means of getting a horse to pay attention to a trainer and also to let the horse work off some energy before anyone rides.) After longeing her for twenty to thirty minutes, Linda was ready to mount Synomi for the first time.

"I got on her, and she was pretty frantic. She just took off. I didn't know at the time but, at the race track, they sometimes slap horses on the side of the neck to get them to go faster. I had learned to slap horses on the side of the neck to get them to pay attention to me! So whap! Whap! I slapped her hard, and she flew, faster, faster, as she had been taught. The other thing I didn't know was that jockeys often pull back on the reins and hold them tight to keep control of the horse while they gallop. That means you can't stop a galloping racehorse simply by pulling back on the reins and screaming 'whoa!' I didn't know this."

Synomi, trained to run faster and faster, ran away with Linda who, until this moment, had never been so fully at the mercy of a totally out-of-control animal. There was no stopping her, only hanging on for dear life. "She eventually decided to stop," Linda sighs, "when she was ready. I had nothing to do with it." Synomi was a horse who interpreted having someone on her back as a signal to run as fast as possible. It seemed Linda had gotten herself a racing machine, not a companion.

But the relationship was just beginning. For the next six months or so, Linda worked with Synomi on the ground—not attempting to ride her. "She was the first and only horse I have ever had to spend that much time with on the ground, without even attempting to mount. I had to spend months not only longeing Synomi but, even more importantly, watching her, observing her every motion and mood." During this period, Linda tried repeatedly to make Synomi submit by doing what she, as a trainer, had learned from other trainers—to whip and punish the horse into submission. "It's the only relationship with a horse I've ever had that I now would describe as abusive," Linda reflects.

This abusive dynamic characterizes most of our encounters with "otherness." We try to dominate, we force submission, we fight because we are afraid of the stranger, the alien, the other. Reflecting this spirit of alienation, people in most cultures around the world assume the right to dominate horses any way they can. According to this logic of domination and submission, horses, like all animals and creatures, exist for human use. This means that horses, like dogs, cows, and other creatures—including subordinate peoples—can be treated any way that dominant peoples wish to treat them. The kindest among dominant humans have always tried to find ways to "break" or domesticate others with as little pain and fear as possible.

But horses are different in an important way from other animals, like dogs, that we "tame." Horses are by nature fear-based animals who will flee when frightened by a sudden noise or motion, by a whip, by pain or the fear of pain. If they cannot flee, they will fight. Using the horse's very nature against it, racehorse owners and trainers often rely on this primal fear and flight pattern as a basic tool in teaching horses to run, the faster the better. From Linda's perspective today, using fear to generate flight as the basis of horse racing is abusive. She learned this lesson from Synomi.

Linda tried to conquer this horse. She tried to whip her into shape. She tried wearing her down through excessive work. She did everything she knew to make the mare submit to her will, but to no avail. Synomi's response was simply to take it. Unlike many horses, Synomi wouldn't fight back—but she also would not submit to Linda. She would not be conquered. She would not be brought around through pain or fear of pain and she would not conquer Linda by hurting her or frightening her. Today Linda speaks of Synomi, whom she calls "Nomi," with great love and respect: "I had to either give up on her or figure out a different way to do it."

In order to do it differently, Linda had to follow where Nomi led. She had to listen and observe. She had to wait for Nomi to be ready to learn from her. Linda sees now that Nomi was also waiting for Linda to be ready to learn from her. They were waiting for each other.

Over the next five years, by figuring out how to do it differently together, Nomi and Linda gave each other many gifts. Linda gave Nomi a new experience of human respect and human patience. Nomi gave Linda a new experience of a horse waiting patiently for a human to learn how to relate to the horse. By refusing to submit to a whip or other gestures of human control, and by not fighting with Linda, Nomi invited Linda to become a more mature equestrian, one who learned through this relationship that she must follow the lead of each particular horse to know how to teach the horse, how to respect and thereby love the horse.

Almost a decade later, Linda says that Nomi taught her that all good relationships, not just human-horse ones, are based in mutuality. "Until people come to this realization, they cannot have good relationships with their horses." "Actually," she continues, "until people come to this realization, they cannot have good relationships with each other. This is what Nomi taught me.

"I was the only person who could ever ride her in a relaxed way—with both Nomi and me relaxed," Linda says. "But I think I gave her an acceptance of people. I gave her an ability to allow people to ride her even though neither they nor she could be as relaxed as she and I learned to be together."

Like humans, horses have personalities, spirits, and souls, the meeting place of Creator and creature, in which energy for mutuality is generated. Humans who want to get to know horses need to respect the horse's soulfulness as well as their own human soulfulness, which is their capacity for relational mutuality and joy. To respect and love a horse is to become aware of the unique personality and spirit of the particular creature. Only in this way can anyone become an excellent equestrian. It has much more to do with quality of relationship than with riding techniques.

To respect and love another person, group, or any creature is to become aware of the unique personality and spirit of the creature. Only in this way can we live with an "other" in a spirit of mutuality, which is always our most moral and surest spiritual foundation. Living in this way has much more to do with the quality of our relationships as groups, individuals, nations, and cultures than with any set of religious or moral rules.

Nomi brought Linda to an awareness of the power of mutual relation. From this point on, Linda was clear that, if she is going to teach people how to ride horses, she must always be learning from the horses what they can teach her and the people who are going to ride them. Every horse is different, and every rider too. If the goal is to help horse and human experience mutuality, teaching becomes an unending process of helping horses and humans discover what each particular horse and human can best learn together and do together and be together.

Linda discovered that Nomi had "a big heart" for both running and people. She loved to run and she really loved it that people enjoyed watching her run. "It was amazing to me that something that beautiful could love and respect me," Linda smiles and pauses. "I don't know exactly what I gave her, but I like to think she experienced, in a horsey way, something similar—that a human being really loved and respected her."

About five years after purchasing Synomi, and with much sadness, Linda traded her for a pony since she was beginning a riding school for kids and needed a few smaller horses. She figured that since she was the only person who could really ride Nomi well, she couldn't justify keeping her because space and money were needed for the others.

"I've come to regret it though," Linda reflects. "After all, I was her person."

Fearing the Other

One of the things about horses that draws us to them is their "otherness" from us and from most other animals that we know well, or think we know well, like cats and dogs. The size and stunning strength of horses can be foreboding. Their personalities may seem elusive and mysterious to us. Horses often stand back (except at feeding time!) and keep their distance even from folks they trust. They often tend to prefer one another's company rather than the company of humans, even humans they trust. Yet some of us feel invited to bridge these differences, to reach through the otherness and connect.

It is interesting to me that so many girls and women seem to be drawn to horses. Linda says she first remembers, at about age ten, thinking how beautiful they are. I remember being amazed and thrilled, as a summer camper, also at about age ten, that something so big could be so gentle, nudging me and nibbling from my hand.

We were girl children seeking a passage through difference in a world in which differences and otherness often seem such an impediment to love. We humans, after all, are a narcissistic species. Humans and horses are alike in this way—drawn to ourselves and those like us, fearing and either fleeing or fighting those who are different from us in ways that we imagine matter. Among humans this fear of otherness is called "xenophobia."

Racism is a hateful form of xenophobia and, in these times, like most others, the world is at risk because of the religious xenophobia of Christians, Jews, Muslims, Hindus, and all others who suppose that "our way" is the only way to live and worship. There is also sexism and its twin, heterosexism, massive evils rooted in the fear of women and sexual mutuality on the part of those men who have ruled the world for centuries and shaped its major religious traditions both West and East. Sexism breeds violence and abuse against women and girls. So why, in this exceedingly dangerous context, are women and girls drawn to horses?

Sometimes it seems as if we have been called together by those voices of ancestors and spirits of humans and horses that know us better than any religious system or man-made god can ever hope to.

When Angela and I first began taking riding lessons from Linda in the spring of 2000, we were sitting behind a Plexiglas window watching several young girls ride beautifully. Beside us, the mother of one of the girls was talking with the father of another. "Don't you ever worry?" she asked. "I mean, don't you ever think about Christopher Reeve?" Without missing a beat, the father responded, "You know, I believe my daughter's in greater danger at church than on that horse." A knowing glance passed between Angela and me.

Could it ironically be for our *safety* that we are called to horses? Do horses invite us to come closer so that we can touch our strength? Do some girls and women, and sometimes boys and men too, intuit something in relation to horses—an energy between us to be shared, a resource of personal and, potentially, social empowerment? A Spirit to be gathered up and embodied by us together? Is this why horses are not simply beautiful, but so compelling, to some of us? Is it why their thundering hooves beat strongly in our own hearts?

Is this what many Native peoples have known from the beginning? That what is Sacred can be shared and in fact must be shared if it is truly Sacred—a liberating energy generated between us not in spite of our otherness but because of, and through, it? Is this what it means to god—to embody this Spirit together and, with and through an-other, to become more fully ourselves because we stretch one another spiritually?

Can we see that we do not need to "break" horses to be safe with them? Can we learn to think differently about how we ask others to meet us, and in what kind of spirit? Can we imagine inviting horses into mutuality with us? Can we learn how really to respect horses, which involves accepting and affirming them in their otherness, rather than assuming that they can, or should, think or act like we do?

Can we also imagine that, in respecting that which is different from us, we humans can be healed from much distress? Can we see that, embodying and representing otherness, horses can soothe injuries laid upon us by human violence and abuse? It may seem odd to us, or it may not, but if God is our power in mutual relation, then the more fully mutual we are able to be with one another—across chasms of species as well as among ourselves as humans—the more deeply rooted in God we become. Mutual relation becomes our healing balm.

Meeting Sugar Meeting Me

The old horse Sugar has drawn me into new depths of otherness. She's helped me begin to learn from other creatures more about the mutuality I've been writing and thinking about for decades, especially in relation to humans, God, and the social order. It all began over the fence in the summer of 1999 in the mountains of western North Carolina.

If she were human, we would call her a "survivor" because Sugar has known some abuse, maybe a lot, over the span of her already long life. Somewhere in her early thirties, Sugar is both a dominant mare and a comic, a steely old girl with soft maternal instincts. I'm told by her former owners that she used to take over the care of calves born to the cows in the pasture where she lived as the only horse. Over the four years I've known Sugar, she's taught me much about otherness. Through the differences between us, Sugar's shown me how little prepared I've been to accept differences and let them be rather than trying in some way to ignore, minimize, or erase them.

Sugar is a special combination of affection and indifference. Almost from the beginning, Sugar liked me. After all, I brought her apples every morning and hung out with her. She would come trotting up to our neighbor's fence when I called and she nuzzled me when I climbed over the fence to join her. Once she ate the apple from my hand and poked around to make sure there wasn't more where it came from, she turned away and meandered off into the pasture, glancing back at me occasionally.

The summer of 1999 was my "Sugar time." It's when she and I met and began to cultivate our relationship. It was a time for me to begin to be aware of how unlike anything or anyone I'd known before this Sugar was. And perhaps the same was true for her.

Every morning I'd head down the hill and through the woods from my home to the pasture where Sugar grazed alongside about a half dozen cows and a bunch of chickens. I didn't know why I was so drawn to this horse. There was nothing special about Sugar, except that she was there and so was I and that seemed to be enough for us both. Once I began to know her, I couldn't resist visiting her daily, so strong was the pull, the invitation to come closer.

What I found in Sugar was a listening buddy. At first, I literally talked to her—"Hi, Sug, how are you today?" Within a couple of weeks, my "language" had become considerably less verbal. Sugar and I would simply be there together, me seated on a log, she standing beside me, the two of us communicating. I knew how she was, and she knew how I was doing too. We were able to "read" each other even though our native cultures and languages were significantly different: I didn't know it at the time, but I would later find out that Sugar's world had been harsh; she'd been ridden with a saddle with a nail poking down into her withers and she had been whipped into running every time her owner mounted her. I could tell, from the outset of our relationship, however, that Sugar was a forgiving and patient animal. I could also tell that Sugar knew that, despite our differences, I was willing to wait with her as we worked out this new relationship.

It took me some time to see that Sugar's forbearing spirit was taking a different shape from mine. While my eyes were following every movement of her eyes, ears, and legs, Sugar was watching me not so much with her eyes as her brain. While most of the time she seemed not to be watching, I began to realize how alert Sugar was to my presence, how aware of my movements, and increasingly how tuned in to my being. I began to notice that, on certain mornings, Sugar would position herself closer to me than at other times. One day, as I was sitting on a log, preoccupied with a personal matter of some sort and not paying much attention to Sugar, I looked up and there she was, standing over me in the manner of a large equine angel, keeping watch.

I stood up, patted her neck and thanked Sugar for being with me. She glanced at me, then down at the coffee cup in my hand and took a big slurp. I laughed and thought I noticed a smile on Sugar's face. Divided by the limits of species, we were joined in that cup of coffee.

CARTER AND RED. "UNTIL YOU WORK THROUGH YOUR FEAR, RED'S GOING TO TEST YOU," LINDA SAID.
"AS LONG AS YOU'RE AFRAID OF THIS HORSE, SHE'S GOING TO SCARE YOU."

Three *Fear*
Shrinking Spiritually

Is there in each of us a capacity for joy and courage that is stronger than fear? Our fear shrinks us spiritually. It diminishes our abilities to deal creatively with what we fear. Our fear of animals, like our fear of people and cultures who are "other," generates even stronger fear. What can we learn from our fear? What can it teach us? Might our fear not have the final word?

Scared of My Own Horse

From the beginning, I experienced my old mare Sugar as a sweet, gentle-spirited companion, a special kind of soul-friend. I heard from a couple of our neighbors who'd tried to ride Sugar that she was not easy to ride. "Difficult" was the word they used. I knew so little about horseback riding, however, that I hadn't a clue what they meant. I figured that, because Sugar and I had begun forging a strong bond, I would certainly be able to ride her—although I was afraid even to try until I could find an arena or small fenced in area in which to do it.

In August 1999, my friend Veheda offered to let me board Sugar in her pasture until we could get a fence built around the meadow on our property. I bought Sugar, moved her to Veheda's farm, and asked Sandi, another friend who is a fine riding instructor, if she would give me some lessons. But even before my lessons could start, I wanted to try riding Sugar, so I decided to begin working with her in Veheda's small round pen rather than her larger riding arena. It felt safer to me.

From day one, I was both drawn to Sugar and frightened. I asked Veheda when she would be home, so that I could ride when she was on the property. I didn't even want to mount Sugar unless someone was around, in case I got into trouble. How could I love this horse, know for sure that she liked me, and still be terrified to get on her back?

Some of my fear had roots in simple body-wisdom. I was fifty-four years old and neither terrifically fit nor athletic in my adult life. I was not initially frightened of Sugar herself but rather of my own awkwardness. I was afraid of falling off and being hurt. Some of my fear simmered in my not knowing what I was doing and in the likelihood of my having little or, God forbid, no control over Sugar's behavior and getting tossed to the ground or run into a tree. Some of my fear was also a fear of otherness and the unknown, a fear of stepping out with this sweet, friendly, and (to me) very large creature into a new, shared adventure.

Lessons in Ignorance and Arrogance

We were able to bring Sugar back home in January 2000. We had built a small barn and had fenced as much pasture as we had at the time, which was not much. To our delight, a young family who was renting a house from us purchased a small Appaloosa horse named Yogi who was able to join Sugar as a resident of the new barn and pasture. This was great because, as herd animals, horses thrive on each other's companionship.

In early January my departure for Massachusetts to begin teaching spring semester at the seminary was still a few weeks off. I'd been taking riding lessons all fall from Sandi and was feeling reasonably confident with Sugar at a walk and trot. I'd fallen off only once, with a couple of bruises and sore muscles to show for it. Although a little reluctant to ride her outside an arena, I wanted to try. I felt like Sugar and I had such a solid relationship that she and I could figure out what to do. I also knew beyond a doubt that Sugar would not intentionally hurt me, and that mattered to me as much as anything.

One morning, coffee in hand, I went down to the barn and spent a leisurely hour grooming Sugar, letting her sip coffee at her pleasure. During this grooming, I was girding up my chutzpah and deciding that this was the day I would ride Sugar up the road and around the property. So I tacked her up, mounted, and began walking her up the dirt road that winds through a pine forest and eventually, after about a mile, comes back round in a circle to the barn. For the first quarter of a mile or so, everything seemed fine, though I was scared—hence, uptight and no doubt sending fear signals to Sugar. Since everything seemed okay, however, I decided that we would trot. So I asked Sug to trot and, here too, she seemed fine. She was listening to me and I was paying careful attention to her, or so I thought.

As a matter of fact, I was paying attention to Sugar. But I didn't know, given my lack of experience with horses, what to look for in Sugar's body and behavior. I didn't know how to assess the "other" in this case. I didn't know how to interpret her ears, nostrils, the carriage of her head, the way her legs were moving, the amount of sweat on her body. How often this is the case! How often we do not know how to interpret the appearances, attitudes, and behavior of those whose cultures, ways of thinking and acting, or species we really do not know very well. Yet how often we think we do know. How often we think we know what we're doing when we haven't a clue.

Without any idea that Sugar was agitated and revving up, I decided that, since everything seemed just fine to me—she had walked and trotted just as I had asked her to—I could let her canter. The canter, for the reader who may not know, is a faster gait than a trot. The canter is often smooth and the gait of choice for pleasure riders who want their horses to run—but not to gallop, which is the fastest, racing gait. But I had not cantered with Sugar before—and had not cantered at all for years.

A little scared but mainly confident that all would be well, I gave Sugar what I thought was the "canter signal," and "Kaboom!" off she shot like a bat out of hell. My feet came out of the stirrups, and my body was tossed up and down and bounced from side to side. I grabbed Sugar's mane with one hand and, with the other, pulled back as hard as I could with both reins and yelled, "Whoa! Whoa! Stop! Stop, Sugar!" To no avail. Sugar galloped faster and faster. I remember seeing a pile of big rocks at the side of the road as we flew by and thinking, "Either I stay on this horse, or I die!" My hands grasped her mane tighter and my legs wrapped for dear life around her body. Fortunately for me, my friend Sugar had no desire to hurl me off her back, because she could easily have run me into trees or bucked me off. All she wanted to do was run faster and, in some sense, I believe, win. So on she raced against the wind, against herself, against the world, against me. Sugar was committed to winning, and I was just as committed to living, so she ran, and I stayed with her, until finally (only a minute later, I'm sure) she stopped sharply and suddenly at my companion Bev's front porch.

Instantly, I leapt to the ground. My heart was racing. I was almost in tears. My body was shaking. I couldn't speak. Often we get through whatever we must and only in the aftermath of a frightening experience do we actually *feel* afraid. This is what happened to me. I had been a little afraid before and during the first part of the ride. Then, as something really frightening happened, all of my psychic energy shot immediately into crisis mode. There was no psychic space in me to feel afraid because all my energy was needed to cope. The moment the crisis was over, however, the fear set in big time and, for the first time, as I landed feet first on the ground and safe, I felt terrified of Sugar and of riding.

What was I afraid of? Several things—not knowing what I was doing, an out of control horse, falling off, being killed. A person who isn't afraid of these things is either stupid or crazy. But, at a more foreboding level, which I knew I needed to explore if I had any desire to keep connecting with horses, my fear was of Sugar's "otherness." In my ignorance of horses—reinforced by arrogance and a lack of humility—I literally had not understood Sugar's body language. I had been so enthralled with my own desire to canter and my confidence in my ability to ride that I had failed to comprehend the level of Sugar's agitation and excitement. There was no way this horse was going to simply canter. Given permission, which is what Sugar interpreted the canter signal to be, Sugar would go as fast as possible. It never occurred to her that I couldn't stay with her.

To ever feel comfortable riding and not be scared each time I mount, I realized that very day that I needed to know a lot more about horses—their language, their culture and habits, how they differ from us humans. It was not Sugar's fault that I was terrified after that ride. It was my own fault for taking Sugar's language, culture, and history (about which I knew little) for granted. Henceforth, I would have to slow down enough in relation to horses—on the ground and on their backs—to get to know them in their "horseness," their "otherness," their particular ways of "speaking" to us humans.

My fear of Sugar was the beginning of any wisdom I might tap in relation to horses, a wisdom that increasingly would shed bright light on our human arrogance in relation to the rest of creation and our appropriate place in it, a place neither too large nor too small.

My first task, in the aftermath of this ride and the terror it stirred in me, was to get back on Sugar the next day and try to do it differently. I wanted to pay more careful attention to see if, this time, I could understand my horse's body language. To my surprise and delight, I found that I could. I found that Sugar wanted to have her own way, which was to trot slowly with me up through the pine trees in the forest, and that she was careful in her steps so as not to bump me into trees or branches. I was not afraid at all, and neither was Sugar.

I was also not in control of my horse. She was taking me where she wanted to go and, happily for me, she didn't mind having me along for the ride. At the other side of the forest, I discovered that I didn't know how to get Sugar to turn around to go back to the barn. I knew technically how to steer a horse, but Sugar had no desire to go back to the barn and wouldn't respond to the reins or my legs. She wanted to go on toward the next forest or field to explore, and I was afraid to try to make her listen to me.

My fear was back. This time I was afraid to insist that Sugar listen to me just as I had been listening to her. I was scared that, if I began to ask her to mind me, to signal her more forcefully with the reins, or my legs, or my voice, she would take off with me again. So I dismounted and walked her back to the barn. While I had spared myself the possibility of another terrifying ride, I knew that this time a combination of fear and inexperience had impeded my ability to figure out my alternatives. Could I have stayed on and successfully insisted that Sugar take me back to the barn? Was I a good enough rider to have done this? Was hopping off the horse my only sane choice in the moment? Was I more afraid than I needed to be?

The problem was not, and never is, that we are scared of things that can hurt us. It is wise to be afraid whenever we are in harm's way. The problem is that, much more often than we realize, we are hounded and haunted by fear that is much larger than it needs to be. And this unnecessary fear is frequently steeped in our ignorance or inexperience with a situation or person, an animal or group, a culture or religion that we don't know very well.

My unnecessary fear of Sugar was really a fear of "otherness," a fear rooted in a combination of my inexperience and ignorance as a horsewoman and my arrogance as a human being. Horses, beginning with Sugar, have taught me that, if we want to encourage one another to move through our fears creatively, we need to realize how inexperienced and ignorant we often are in relation to persons and creatures that frighten us. We also need to confess our deep hubris, our false pride and arrogance, as human beings who imagine that we know most of what there is to know about what will harm us and what will keep us safe.

CALCULATED RISKS

Looking up,
I see
danger
and a sign
that says
equestrian activities are inherently
dangerous
and that it's nobody's fault
but your own
if you're hurt
or killed.

But
a young man
watching his daughter ride
says she's in less danger
on a horse
than in church.

I know what he means
but still I ask Linda,
"why do you take such a risk?"

"Because," she says,
"it's what gives me life."

I ask if she's afraid
of her horse Levi.
"Of course." She nods,
"He's huge and he's young."

Helping people work through their fear of horses including, sometimes, their own horses, is one of Linda's strengths as a teacher. It's something she began to learn from Mike, her first horse, given to her by a Vermont farmer when she was about twelve.

Mike was a big horse and Linda adored him. "He was also too much horse for me at the time. I was a beginner and he used to buck me off and run away with me." Linda recalls and laughs, "That horse gave me a good, healthy respect for the danger of being with horses.

"Mike taught me to have fear and how to be afraid. Looking back on it now, I see that the experience with him helped me become empathic with people who're afraid of horses, even their own. I understand that someone can absolutely love an animal and still be scared to death of it. I learned this from Mike.

"That horse also taught me what it meant to realize that I don't know what I'm doing, that I need to do it differently, or get help, or stop doing it. This lesson has served me well as a teacher and a trainer and, I guess, as a person!"

Linda continues, "Today I take only calculated risks with horses. If I know I'm going to be in a situation in which I'm going to feel a lot of fear toward a horse, I won't put myself in that situation. I'll do whatever I need to do with other horses or with the help of particular people before I try to work with a horse that really scares me, and sometimes I'll decide that it's just not going to work, a particular horse and me.

"That's because if you approach a horse with fear, whatever the problem is between you and the horse will only escalate. The horse will either dominate you, because she (let's say she's a mare) knows you're afraid or, if you're connected with her, she'll take on your fear as her own. So she'll either have an aggressive response to you or a fear response with you and neither is a good thing.

"If she does sense your fear, you have to work it through with her. You have to see that it's your problem—this fear—as much as hers and that the two of you have to work through the fear together. Otherwise, your relationship with the horse is not going to be good."

When I asked Linda how she works with folks who are afraid of their own horses, she smiled at me and nodded knowingly. "The first thing you do is help them get the facts and see what they're actually working with. When you're dealing with fear, it helps to get clear-headed and be realistic about what you're scared of. Remember how it was with you and Red?"

As Long as You're Afraid, the Horse Will Scare You

In January 2001, Angela and I arrived back in Massachusetts for the winter and spring, me to teach at the seminary and she to work in a parish. We brought Red, the quarter horse, with us because Linda had agreed to work with Red and us.

I had bought Red the previous summer from a woman in North Carolina who, it turns out, had been afraid of her. Although Angela and I had been drawn to Red from the moment we met her, we had learned pretty quickly that she is a strong, willful mare who wants her own way—so much so that, over the six months Red had been with us in North Carolina, we had become wary of her behavior: Often she would rear up a little and dance around if her rider wanted her to go one way and she wanted to go another. Whenever this happened, the rider had to fight with Red to get her to obey—and, in relation to me, Red would usually win.

Her behavior was disconcerting enough to me that I usually would dismount and make Red walk alongside me in the direction I wanted to go. A couple of our more experienced equestrian colleagues tried riding Red and she did the same thing with them. This scared them to the point that they advised us not to ride Red at all until we, or someone, could correct her behavior. Angela and I decided to hang out with Red and work with her on the ground until we could get her up to our teacher Linda in Massachusetts.

Looking back, Angela and I admitted that neither of us was scared enough to stop riding Red even temporarily, or to stop trying to work through whatever was happening. But when our more seasoned equestrian colleagues told us that we really should be scared because Red's behavior was dangerous—a rearing horse is a dangerous horse because she can go over and come down on top of the rider—Angela and I both became more frightened. We were baffled because Red did not seem to either of us to be any more dangerous than any other basically kind horse. We knew Red was connected with both of us in special ways—and we did not believe she would ever try to harm us. Still we didn't want to be foolhardy and we didn't want to get hurt. So we stayed off Red until we got back to Massachusetts.

One morning in early February we sat on bleachers with our hot coffee, huddled under blankets in the indoor arena in Littleton, Massachusetts, to watch Linda work with Red. For the first twenty minutes or so we watched them together on the ground, Linda walking up to Red and talking softly to her, touching the side of her head, walking around her, touching her body—side, haunches, tail. It all seemed to be in slow motion. Then, still on the ground, Linda "longed" Red—working with her on a long lead, getting her to move on voice command: "walk, halt, walk, trot, walk, halt, walk, trot, canter, trot, walk, halt."

This ground work, I was learning, is an important part of building a relationship with any horse. You don't just hop on and take off. You have a relationship to build with another creature, in which you have to get to know each other as the particular character each of you is. This introductory work, which we do not just once but again and again, is especially important in any relationship in which either or both parties are afraid. As Linda had told us, in the horse-human relationship, whenever the human is afraid, the horse is also, because horses catch and carry their human's feelings. A scared human means a scared horse, and this can be a bad combination.

Through the ground work, Linda was getting to know Red and, as importantly, Red was getting to know Linda. Perhaps each of their fears was abating? In any case, each was having a chance to get a "feel" for the other. The introduction complete, the ride could begin.

From the beginning, the sight of Linda riding Red has been like watching a pair of dancers in a ballet, moving together rhythmically, purposefully, playfully, Red with her unusually smooth gaits and Linda in her exquisite confidence. For ten minutes or so, this first ride was smooth and sweet. Then, all of a sudden, despite their connection and Linda's gentle direction, Red decided to veer off to the left and, when Linda resisted, proceeded to rear up in protest. Using her leg, seat, hands, and voice together, Linda immediately corrected Red, bringing her quickly back onto the course they had been navigating together, and they continued on their way. A few minutes later, it happened again, and Linda, again responding instantly with all four "natural aids"—leg, seat, hands, voice—brought Red back into line. The pattern continued for another fifteen or twenty minutes: from a steady, easy ride to disruption and correction, then back to the steady, easy ride.

Linda rode Red over to Angela and me and asked us what we had been noticing.

We said we noticed how unflappable Linda seemed in this situation. We noticed that her correction of Red's behavior was clear, firm, and forceful, yet did not seem angry or harsh. We noticed that Linda's response to Red's misbehavior did not seem to either frighten or anger Red but rather simply to let her know what she, Linda, expects of Red. "You bet," Linda said, "if we're going to get along, she needs to know that I expect her to listen to me."

"But did her behavior scare you?" I wanted to know, thinking of the rearing up and what I'd been warned about—the possibility that Red could go over backwards with the rider on board!

Linda asked if Red's rearing up with us had been like what she'd done with her—popping up twelve inches or so.

"I think so," I nodded, and Angela agreed, "No, daahling, she doesn't go up higher than that."

"Then you don't have to worry," Linda said. "She's not going to go up and over—it's not in her conformation (the way she's built) and it's not in her attitude. Red's got a strong will. She can be stubborn. And she's testing you. But there's not a mean bone in this horse's body. You've got a horse who's basically kind and wants to please you, but who's also testing you to see what you're going to allow—and to see if you're going to be afraid of her."

"Until you work through your fear, Red's going to test you," Linda mused as she dismounted. "I mean it," she spoke emphatically to Angela and me, "As long as you're afraid of this horse, she's going to scare you."

Horse ethics:
When in danger, flee.
If you can't,
then fight.

Patriarchal ethics:
When in danger, fight.
If you can't,
then flee
(if you can).

Horses and humans are born into fear, some of it important in positive ways, a key to our survival: fear of anything that will eat us up, for instance, and fear of abuse and violence. But much of our fear—especially of the unknown and the other, the stranger and the new—is an impediment to our vitality, joy, and ability to love deeply. Learning our way through fear is a primary challenge for humans and horses. For humans, at least, it is a *spiritual* challenge. Horses can help teach us courage by accompanying us through the fear just as we accompany them.

A truly mutual connection between human and horse is one in which each is becoming more empathic, more finely attuned, to the other's way of being. When either is afraid, the other also experiences fear. But if the relationship is strong, they can move together through the fear toward a shared sense of greater safety, each encouraging the other.

"It's What Gives Me Life"

Why do we risk harm, even death, by riding horses?

Linda says it's what gives her life.

Is it simply the act itself, doing something dangerous, that produces a rush of energy that feels, to Linda and others, like life itself? For many equestrians and other sports folk, it may be simply the thrill, the danger, knowing that, even under the best conditions, we are not totally in charge.

For others, it may be more. It may be not simply the inherent danger, but moreover a relational quality, a power for growth and confidence, that can be experienced as life because this power for relationship *is* the source of life itself.

Is this why the most serious climbers scale Everest? Is it what draws seasoned sailors out to sea? Is it why many athletes jump and dive, ski and race in death-defying matches? Could it even be why soldiers who are committed to peacemaking, soldiers bearing compassion, put themselves in harm's way? Are these men and women yearning for some sacred power in relation to mountain, water, earth, humans, other creatures? And is this power they seek sacred precisely because it is in some way "mutual," shared among the elements that constitute life itself?

Does the most experienced climber realize the mountain's power to relate? Do the sailors and soldiers sense themselves pulled by sea and comrades, drawn sometimes even by their enemies, more fully toward glimpses of life itself, which can happen, perhaps, in a flash at death's door? For what do people take such calculated risks? Could it be to see the face of God? Is this what people are yearning for when they risk even their lives for experiences of right relation with lover or mountain, cherished friend or dreaded enemy, persons of different cultures or religions, children or elders, ocean or air, dog or ape, elephant or horse?

Without a doubt it is dangerous to be around horses and to get close to them. It is dangerous and we are wise to be afraid and to shrink spiritually into a knowledge of who we really are, who we are not, and what our place is. But we humans and horses can encourage one another through fear and, with one another's help, we can grow larger and more beautiful than we have been before.

We might also keep in mind that we live in danger, all of us, and much more so from the absence of mutuality in our public and private lives than from any horse or person, species or group that differs from us in language or culture. In our context of perpetual danger, horses as spiritual teachers can be a resource for our empowerment and safety.

ANGELA AND RED.
"DAAHLING," ANGELA WOULD SAY,
"THERE'S NOTHING LIKE A HORSE
TO TEACH YOU WHAT'S REALLY IMPORTANT!"

Four *Balance*
Sitting Deep and Well

For horses and humans alike, balance is the foundation of a healthy and happy life. Balance is not a wishy-washy, lukewarm "neutrality." It is not a refusal, or inability, to take a stand. Balance is a capacity to bend, let go, sit deep, and go with the energy. In relation to each other, neither horse nor rider can relax without balance, and neither is safe. For a few riders, achieving balance seems to come as naturally as it does for most horses. For most of us, however, achieving balance on a horse—as in life itself—is challenging. Becoming a balanced rider is a long-term goal requiring lots of patience on the part of the person and the horse.

A Holy Matter

From the beginning, Angela was a balanced rider. At least that's what Linda and the rest of us imagined as we watched her with Red.

Sister Angela, as she was known professionally in her native Australia, was in her early seventies when she resumed horseback riding after more than forty years "enclosed" in a contemplative Anglican convent. Born in 1926 to a country doctor and his wife, Wendy Hope Solling (later, "Sister Angela") had often accompanied her father on horseback into the backcountry of New South Wales to visit his patients. A blurry photo of Wendy at about age twelve shows her astride a massive horse. Wendy's long back and neck are extended energetically upward and her legs are caressing the horse's body in what appears to be a gentle rhythm. It's a picture of a thin, gangly kid with pigtails totally at ease on the back of a horse whose own energy is also evident. The horse is ready to go, but his ears and posture convey an attentiveness to Wendy; he is waiting with her.

In 1999, following a series of "mini-strokes," Sister Angela decided to leave Australia, at least for a while, to join Sue, Bev, and me in our small community in western North Carolina. Angela arrived a few months after I had purchased the old mare Sugar from our neighbor and she was ecstatic to meet this latest, and only equine, member of the family.

"Daahling," she would say, "there's nothing like a horse to teach you what's really important." Thereupon, Angela set out sharing memories of her childhood on horseback and showing us photographs of wire sculptures she had made of drovers, horsemen in the Australian outback, during her brief career as a sculptor before she entered the Clare Community at age twenty-nine. Not only as an animal person—a horse person in particular—but also as an artist, Angela had long loved the horse's form, the rhythm of its movement, its flowing mane and tail, the sound of its hooves, its beauty—in a word, its balance.

Once, as we stood at the fence watching Sugar and our neighbors' Appaloosa pony Yogi run alongside each other at the other side of the pasture, Angela said that horses reminded her of God's movement among us: strong, intimidating, frightening, yet beautiful, inviting, and in some strange way comforting.

Simply to observe them is to marvel in realizing that, as a species, these great creatures' lives are intimately connected with our own humanity. Here in the United States and elsewhere, horses have been our helpers, an indispensable economic resource over time. Like God, they have been our good friends, steadfast companions, even our saviors and also, like God, they have been objects of our greed, abuse, and exploitation.

In January 2000, Angela and I traveled back north to study and work. About a month later we began our lessons with Linda. For these lessons over the next three months, I leased a horse, Mary Lou, and Angela rode an especially sweet quarter horse named Smudge. For me, it was a time of developing nascent riding skills, a challenging effort since I am not a "natural rider" like Angela and Linda, and I was also still leery from my out-of-control rides on Sugar in North Carolina only a couple of weeks earlier. For Angela, it was a matter of giving her body a chance to remember what she'd known since child-hood: how to ride a horse and, even more basically, how to connect with the horse while still on the ground.

As much as we both would learn from Linda over the next two years, I learned as much from Angela about some of the ingredients that go into achieving "balance" with and, eventually, on a horse—and in life itself.

Although there is certainly no necessary relationship between one's religion, if any, and how a person relates to other people or animals, a relationship is a *spiritual* transaction. This is because our power to connect in a spirit of radical mutuality with one another is our sacred power, God. Indeed, our inherent connectedness as earth creatures is the Spirit's manifestation among us. In this context, which for Angela was life itself, the relationship with horses was a holy matter. From the outset, Angela simply assumed that the horse would be a God-bearer to her just as she would carry the Spirit into her relationship with the horse. Much as she did with other people, in relation to horses, Angela had faith in the possibility of knowing and being known by the "other." Relationships for her were like stepping through a veil, without clarity or certainty of what she, or the other, would meet on the other side.

"Going riding," she said to me, "is better than going to church." I agreed, especially we noted, when church means shutting our eyes and minds to the presence and power of a God in whom women and men and children and creatures of all cultures and colors and religions and sexualities and other diversities live. Angela and I, even as religious professionals, were among the throngs who have been spiritually battered by the church's sanctimonious moralisms as well as its misogynist treatment of women. We shouldn't have to hide who we are in church: our dreams, our questions, our feelings, how we really live in the world of God. With horses, as with God, we *can't* hide who we are. Horses simply know. If you think you're hiding your fear or absentmindedness or pain or joy or anything else from a horse-companion, you'll be surprised much as we are when we think we're hiding from God.

So one of the gifts Angela brought to horses—and one of the basic ingredients in her balance—was her faith. Angela's stunning faith in God secured her faith in horses.

There was also her attentiveness. One day, out at the stables in suburban Boston, Angela watched quietly as Linda worked on the ground for at least thirty minutes with Charlie, a horse who was scared of people. Later, Angela asked Linda what she'd been doing with Charlie.

"Just taking my time with him." Linda then explained to us that she had been working intentionally very slowly with Charlie, allowing him to eventually begin to trust her and finally let her touch him and begin, just barely begin, to build his willingness to trust a person.

"This is what I want to be able to do!" Angela declared. "It's what I'm most interested in, not so much the riding, although that's wonderful, but the relationship itself." I thought to myself, that's one of the reasons Angela is already such a good rider. She always takes time simply to watch and listen, to stand alongside the horse for long stretches of time, sometimes talking, sometimes in silence, just letting the horse begin to know her. One of our horsewomen friends, Peg, told us that she sings to her horse, something I have begun with mine. In the meantime, as I watched Angela watching horses, I learned something important about paying attention. *It takes more time than we think we have.* It also requires us to approach the "other" with a mind wide open to what we may discover today.

Then there was Angela's courage, an embodied courage to let go and let the horse carry her. The big mistake most aspiring riders make is the same mistake most of us make in living life itself: we hold on too tight and become rigid. Our minds get set, and our bodies get stiff and contorted and, if we fall, we usually get hurt. By the time Angela got on Smudge, and later Red, she was ready to let the horse carry her rather than needing to "control" or "master" the horse.

How did she get to this? Whence does this courage come? Knowing Angela, I am confident it came from her God-secured faith in the horse's capacity to connect with her and also her careful attentiveness—cultivated, from the outset of the relationship, on the ground—to the horse's particular way of being a horse, how it moved, what scared it, what it seemed to notice, what it responded to, what it seemed to enjoy. This depth of attentiveness also helped make Angela a great sculptor.

By the time Angela mounted, the horse Smudge was her friend.

And so, later, was Red.

Angela and Red

When it became clear that Sugar was too old for us to keep riding, Angela and I went with a friend to look at Red as a possible purchase. When we first laid eyes upon "Big Red" she was sparkling in the early morning sun, her light red coat set off by the deeper red of her mane and tail. "But how gorgeous, daahling!" Angela exclaimed.

Angela and I needed a horse that could help us become better riders. The quarter horse Red would become that horse. Over the next eighteen months Angela and I worked with Red. She watched me ride and I watched her and we'd often do our ground work with Red together, each helping the other figure out what to do next or how to interpret what was happening. In North Carolina, where we spent most of our time, we had several knowledgeable mentors. Sandi and Liz were both excellent teachers of balance in complementary and different ways. Their particular gifts as horsewomen were mutually enhancing and Angela and I loved them both and learned from each of them.

Liz helped increase our competence and confidence that we could stay on a moving animal, even if the horse spooked at a deer or a snake. She had us riding bareback, learning to feel Red's body move beneath our legs and seat, cantering up hills and around trees, holding on to the horse's mane if we felt we were losing our balance. Probably more than anyone, Liz was teaching us to love riding. For her, "balance" meant being able to stay on the moving horse.

For Sandi, "balance" was a technical term referring to the quality of "seat" a rider is able to maintain on a horse and also to the horse's ability to walk, trot, or canter smoothly and safely, a capacity strengthened by the rider's "balanced seat." Sandi could teach us the form and skills of European riding cultures. It was with Sandi that we could continue to sharpen basic equestrian skills such as how to hold the reins, where and how to sit in the saddle, where to keep our legs and heels, how to use our natural aids—voice, hands, legs, seat—together, which is no simple thing for most aspiring equestrians.

We also took some lessons in North Carolina with a third gifted equestrian, Alyssa, who helped us especially with ground work. She worked with us to build skills slowly, gently, and methodically in relation to the horse. Alyssa helped us learn more about how to patiently "read" our friend Red in nuanced ways. She suggested that we might interpret Red's renowned stubbornness not necessarily as simply a willful attitude but, perhaps, as Red's way of communicating to us that something was the matter—maybe some pain or maybe some memory of trauma releasing fear. After all, one of Red's former owners had told me by phone shortly after I purchased her that her early training had been at the hands of a woman known in Michigan as "the trainer from hell."

The backdrop to Angela's and my equestrian adventures, including the special relationship we were forging with Red, was the rising social turbulence in the United States and around the world following the 2000 electoral coup and the terrifying events of September 11, 2001, and their aftermath at home and abroad. As an Australian, Angela was shocked by the degree of machismo and hyper-patriotism that fueled the "war against terrorism" here in the United States. She was also disturbed that her own native land was following suit by waging war rather than attempting to build a strong, durable peace in concert with other nations.

During this time, the horses themselves, as well as Free Rein, the therapeutic riding center we had begun in North Carolina, became precious resources for healing and education. It had been my hope when Free Rein began, and it continues to be my hope, that Free Rein someday might be known throughout this part of the country as a peace center, a place where groups and individuals can come to work on social and personal liberation.

Angela had no doubt, and neither did I, that the Spirit of God was calling us to the horses and to Free Rein as resources of Sacred Power, to help us and others seek and find more than we have known before about God, the world, and ourselves.

Red and Angela's Christic Power

In mid-January 2002, Angela and I were packing to head back north to Massachusetts in less than a week. I'd been busy planning my courses, including an introduction to Christology, the study of how Christians believe the humanity and divinity of Jesus are connected. This may not appear to have much to do with horses or therapeutic riding and in most classical Christianity it doesn't, but I was becoming increasingly mindful that animals and other creatures, including earth and sky, have much to teach us about God and the world if our hearts and minds are open. I had become aware that horses, like other created beings, and indeed like Jesus of Nazareth whom Christians call "Christ," have much in common: Their embodied spirits yearn for right, mutual, relation in ways particular to their species as well as their personal histories and characteristics. Often, as with Jesus and many other humans, their capacity to give and receive kindness is met with abuse and violence. Still, in the same one Spirit as the brother from Nazareth, a horse can be a mighty conduit of the power of God for a person seeking liberation.

Angela's faith in the horses, her attentiveness to them, and her courage to let them carry her led to joy in experiencing a sense of abandonment and balance with at least one horse. She had been doing a lot of ground work with Red and a lot of quiet "lateral" work, in which a rider uses primarily her legs, seat, and back to urge a horse to take small steps sideways.

This kind of work with a horse is what many equestrians refer to as "dressage," a form of classical European riding that, in the United States as well as Europe today, tends to convey a high degree of cultural snobbery as well as skill. Linda, Sandi, and Alyssa helped Angela and me understand that dressage is basically about "balance," which requires building a mutual relationship between horse and rider. Its ground work, lateral work, and other aspects of training the horse to step quietly are ways of fine-tuning the balance of both horse and rider, enabling each to better listen to, understand, work, and play with the other. Angela loved doing dressage with Red, and Red was becoming increasingly attentive to Angela.

One early January morning Angela and I headed out on foot toward the stables, which were about a half mile from home. On the way over, she told me she'd like to try to ride in that "same gorgeous way 'our Linda' rides Red." We chuckled, both of us imagining how unlikely it seemed that anyone could ride Red like Linda, whom we had observed time and again connecting with Red, on her back and on the ground, the way a maestro relates to an orchestra, each at its best, in concert.

The weather that day was perfect—probably around 70 degrees F, under a clear blue sky. It was one of those unseasonable January days in the South when riding outside in an arena infused by the stillness and silence of winter filtering through trees that are bare is not only possible but glorious. Sitting there in jeans and a sweatshirt, I watched from the bleachers as Red and Angela began their ride.

The first thing I noticed was how happy both of them seemed. Angela was beaming and Red, in her own horse-way, was letting us know that she too was feeling good—ears forward and at ease, head and neck relaxed, mouth and tongue indicating a willing connection with Angela, legs and body moving softy and rhythmically under Angela, whose own movements were barely perceptible.

"Wow," I thought, and then spoke out loud, "You two are beautiful right now! I mean, you're both always gorgeous but something's going on here—this is really special! Are you aware of this?" I asked from my perch.

Her long back extended upward and her head held high, Angela glanced in my direction, smiled confidently, and nodded, "Yes, daahling."

I'm not enough of an equestrian to describe in detail what I saw, but I can tell you that Red was moving in such a way that her body seemed to be floating. There was not a hint of heaviness or awkwardness, and Angela's embodied energy seemed to reflect Red's elegance. Theologically, I'd say that they were generating this energy together, and that it was sacred.

Then and there, I realized that Angela and Red were becoming one living, moving figure in creation. Angela was indeed riding Red like Linda rides her, perhaps even more beautifully because Angela had come to know and love Red so deeply. They were moving laterally, forward, and backward, walking, trotting, and cantering in what seemed to be slow motion. Red and Angela. Angela and Red. Together, they were one christic body, infused with divine power.

Fifteen or twenty minutes passed, during which I sat transfixed before the theophany—manifestation of the divine—that was unfolding before my eyes. Whatever the Spirit might have been "telling" Angela and Red, I was being shown by the two of them and the Spirit between them something I had never realized before in quite this way: God really does make us one. We really are "one in the Spirit" and this does not negate or diminish our otherness or separateness or diversity. Angela was not becoming a horse, and Red will never be human and yet, together, with one another's help, each was transcending the limits of species and particularity to become more than either could ever be by herself.

For the first time in my life I realized what God was, and is, doing in Jesus and in and through the life of every one who struggles for mutuality with others. This is, for Christians, the meaning of "Christ" or "christic power"—that through which we become one with God and with each other and yet our distinctness, our otherness, the special persons or creatures that each of us is remains intact.

It is how we achieve our balance—as humans, as creatures, all of us shaped by a power that moves through us toward greater mutuality. And the balance we achieve in such powerful relational moments is between our separateness and our unity, between our diversity and our commonality. God lives among us most fully in the spaces between us, where sacred power is generated. To ride, to love, to work, to live in these spaces is to live in the balance that is at the very core of God. When I looked up, they were standing before me, Red and Angela, as still and quiet as the winter forest that was their backdrop. Red looked utterly serene and Angela was all smiles.

"Daahling," she said exuberantly, "this is what I've been waiting for all my life! It has been the perfect ride!"

It was also Angela's last ride. Three days later, Angela had a massive cerebral hemorrhage, and she died peacefully, surrounded by loved ones, on January 20, 2002.

"Ask Me to Ride with You"

Some folks, myself included, believe that Red went into mourning with me and Linda and other of Angela's friends. For the next several months Linda worked with Red and me to help restore my confidence—and maybe Red's too—to carry on together without our beloved friend, yet very much in her spirit. In fact, it took me a couple of months to realize how frightened I was to ride without Angela. I was almost too scared to ride again, though I was giving it my best effort.

One day in March, a couple of months after her death, I had an especially stunning sense of Angela's presence with me and I heard her saying, "Daahling, ask me to ride with you and that gorgeous Red. Ask me to ride with you and you'll both be fine!"

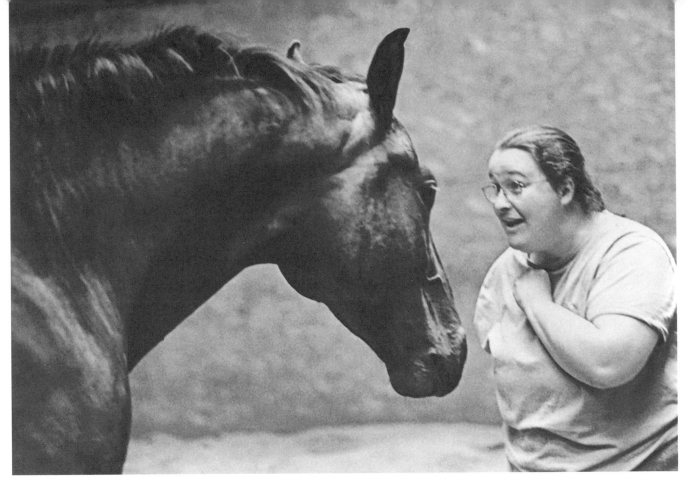

LINDA AND LEVI. COULD OUR DESIRE TO GENERATE AND SHARE BEAUTY,
TO KNOW OTHERS AND BE KNOWN FOR WHO WE REALLY ARE, BE A REFLECTION OF GOD'S IMAGE?

Five *Beauty*
Reflecting Who We Are

Beauty is a quality we recognize in those who recognize it in us. Beauty is not cosmetic, not surface appearance. Sometimes cosmetics can cover our pain, age, secrets, shame, or simply what is real in our lives. Sometimes cosmetics can hide what we cannot face. By contrast, beauty comes in the uncovering of who we really are: joyful, sorrowful, confident, unsure, hopeful, fearful, rested, tired, peaceful, anxious, and all the in-between places. Beauty is a quality rooted in the mutuality of our yearning for connectedness to other creatures and creation itself. It takes shape in the integrity and authenticity of our lives.

In human experience, beauty reflects our values and conveys a sense of whether, and how, the way we live reflects these values. Whether we are human or horse, olive tree or night sky, our beauty reveals how those who love us experience us. In that sense, our beauty reflects the truth of our relational character—who we are to others. Beauty is a confirmation that we fit together, that we are participants in creation, each in our own way, that we have a rightful place in the larger picture, that we belong here, and that it is good that we are here, together.

Cinnamon Joe

The year was 1973. Cinnamon Joe, a strawberry roan pony, needed a child who wanted him, but not just any child. Joe needed someone who could really enjoy his special energy. He needed a good rider, a kid with a passion for riding well. A horse's best human friend is not only kind and respectful but also knows how to sit and move, how to use reins and legs, so as to invite and free the horse to enjoy his own energy. It's like people needing not simply to be treated kindly by other people but, almost as importantly, needing to be empowered through our closest relationships to be our best selves, to have our most creative and liberating energies released so that we can live with purpose and passion. This is what the pony Cinnamon Joe needed: to be able to enjoy his best horse-energies. He needed a child to come along who could do this with him—*someone to recognize his beauty, so that he could become beautiful.*

"And along I came," says Linda. "I was about thirteen. Joe was exactly the pony I needed."

It was with Joe that the young Linda began first to experience herself as a gifted horsewoman, an athlete, most importantly a kid whose yearning for connection to horses—and through them to her own best self—was not a passing phase but was already becoming the center of her life. By the time she was fifteen, Linda was teaching riding and knew that this would be her life's work, really her spiritual vocation, as well as her profession.

Linda and Levi

To most people who watch her with horses, especially her own horse Levi, Linda Levy is a beautiful woman. She is also a big woman in a culture that tells us big women are not beautiful. One of the gifts that horses and many other animal companions offer us is an appraisal of who we are that has little to do with appearance and everything to do with the truthfulness of our lives, who we really are.

Leviticus—called Levi—Linda's horse today, is big, standing almost eighteen hands (six feet) at the withers, which is where his neck meets his back. That means that Linda, at five-feet, four inches, stands eight inches shorter than Levi at the withers. When I asked Linda about this large, black horse she told me that Levi is an "Oldenburger" because he was born in the province of Oldenburg, Germany. Linda found him in 2001—a big, awkward four-year-old, being trained at his breeder's farm in Germany. She was drawn to him more by his personality than his appearance.

Linda smiled as she described the horse she met in Germany. "Levi was soft and knowing at a very young age. What made him special was his real, transparent desire to please the humans in his life, even those he'd just met, like me."

She recalls going into his stall, "Here was this BIG head reaching down to say hello. He had no suspicions or reservations. Just a pure, friendly way about him—a beautiful horse.

"When I look at horses," Linda continued, "there's something I can't describe in words but I know it's there, a quality that makes a horse tractable, able to be handled by average people who may be limited in their horsemanship. I felt Levi had that quality. He has shown me since that he does.

"My first real contact with Levi in the United States was when he got to New York at the quarantine station," she laughed. "People stopped to look at him when I was leading him onto the trailer. It must have been a sight—this little butterball woman leading this giant monster of a horse! I was thinking, 'O God, please let this horse walk onto the trailer because he is so big I could never force him on!' Always a gentleman, Levi simply followed me onto the trailer. He's also an incredible athlete. Strong, supple, and intelligent."

I asked Linda to say more about Levi's beauty, which, from the beginning, clearly meant more to Linda than simply his handsome conformation (shape). She saw the same beauty parents and grandparents see when they think their own babies are the most beautiful in the world.

"I think it has to do with freedom." Linda pauses, then speaks thoughtfully, "And not just Levi's freedom, but mine too, my own potential, a quality in me that he represents to me." She and I discussed whether this sense of "freedom" is a factor in the appeal of horses to so many girls and women. Is it why we find them beautiful? Is it this beauty to which so many girls and women aspire? Do horses show us what we too can be—more importantly, do they show us who we are when we are most fully in touch with our power? In that moment, is there a way in which we too are free and beautiful?

What Would He Name You?

I asked Linda,
can you really know Levi?
not simply how to ride him,
show him, enjoy him,
but really know him
at the core of his
beauty?
And can you let him know
who you really are,

not just the parts of you
that others (and sometimes
even you yourself)
know best?
I said, Linda,
you have named him:
*   "Leviticus" "Levi"*
What would he name you?

Beautiful. *That's what he would name you.*

How often in our society does a big woman think of herself as beautiful? In truth, how often does any strong, intelligent woman think of herself as beautiful in a culture that tells us we are not? How can women, especially large women, imagine ourselves as beautiful when the dominant cultural forces—religion, economy, fashion, and other artifacts of popular consumption—conspire to call big women fat and ugly, even incompetent and stupid?

Like most survivors of this "fat mythology," my friend Linda, how do you feel, even as an equestrian whom so many regard as so very excellent, so much a cut above? What do you, lovely, strong horsewoman, do with all these feelings?

When you turn to Levi, do you feel your preciousness? Is your sense of self transformed? Is this a gift you receive from these beautiful creatures? With the horses, especially Levi, do you become a Big Beautiful Embodied Woman, Bearer of Sacred Power? That is certainly how your students—and surely, even more, those persons most intimately involved with you, like your husband Andy and daughter Hannah—experience you—as supremely competent, alive, and lovely, with an embodied wisdom as old as the hills, lessons you learned with the horses.

As you know, Linda (for you have taught me this), Levi sees you as you are. He knows every muscle in your body, every motion you make, every pound of your bodyself seeking to connect with him in mutually empowering ways, for him, for you. His beauty—his sense of freedom, both realized and often simply a yearning—calls forth yours, and you proudly, boldly step up to meet him in this freedom, do you not?

Although those who see Levi say, "How beautiful!" no one really knows him like you do. And although quite a few people see you as a beautiful woman, no one sees you quite the way Levi does. You know each other's yearnings for freedom and mutuality in ways that only the two of you can touch together. And this is beauty: a quality we touch together, a delight we recognize in those who call it forth in us.

Uncovering Ourselves

In the hustle and bustle of today's world and the clamor and commotion of human society, the yearning for real beauty, its roots deep in mutual relation, may be a common human experience, yet one too often buried beneath the lies and clutter of consumerist capitalism. This yearning for real beauty is something in us all, something we share, yet real beauty is so hard for most of us to reach, because it is hard in this world to simply be ourselves.

Could this yearning, our desire to generate and share beauty, to know others and be known for who we really are, be a reflection of God's image? And could our innocence—our capacity to believe in something wonderful at the core of our being and the yearning it generates—connect us to who other creatures also are at their best? Is this innocence and a yearning for the beautiful freedom of spirit and body "hard wired" into both horses and humans? Is this sense of freedom and beauty a gift we actually share with other creatures, like horses?

Real beauty is soulful. Soul is the meeting place of Spirit and flesh, the meeting place of heaven and earth in us, in which the Spirit yearns to know and be known, to love and be loved, to be brought to life, through us, and recognized, in and with us, as beautiful flesh, beautiful earth. Christians have missed the truth in supposing that humans are the only creatures with such soul. In fact, we humans may well be the creatures whose relation to the Sacred One is the most fraught with ambivalence and resistance. It seems likely that we have more complex souls than most creatures because the Spirit's yearnings for freedom and beauty through us are so compromised by our efforts to cover this up: to hide who we really are from one another, ourselves, and God.

Our beauty grows in the uncovering of ourselves, in which we make known our yearning for right relation, which is God's own yearning, and in which we make known our hunger for God, which is in truth God's hunger for us.

It is no wonder that artists and musicians so often are the chief portrayers of beauty in human life. The best makers of paintings and songs, concertos and pots, poems and films offer us glimpses of ourselves as we really are and as we aspire to be, and that is why we regard their work as great. We sometimes say that we go to the movies "to escape" and perhaps we do, but the films that really stay with us and sometimes even change our lives are the ones that tell us something about ourselves, who we are, who we can be, and that we too are beautiful in ways that we too often fail to notice.

This is why, from early on, I've thought that the best theologians are often the artists among us. It's why I ask my theological students, as well as my horseback riding students, to write poetry, draw pictures, and sing songs. One good way to learn to recognize beauty in others and ourselves is to practice giving it voice or form through putting words, color, shape, and sound "out there" so that we can see it, hear it, touch it, sometimes even taste or smell it—and know that the color or voice or shape is really quite lovely.

But as long as human social life is shaped largely by fear rather than by faith in the human, creaturely, creative, and divine Spirit, our prevailing notions of "beauty" will also be shaped largely by fear. We will wander aimlessly on, lost in vain and collective aspirations for a "beauty" that no one ever finds except fleetingly. In this world, in which we are drawn to "the lifestyles of the rich and famous," there will always be something "countercultural" about real, lasting beauty. Real beauty—the beauty that is freedom and innocence, the beauty that yearns for mutuality and is also born in it—is a quality that irks because it eludes, the rich and famous, the principalities and powers.

Bad Politics, Cosmology, and Theology

In Western civilization, Christian theology has not on the whole been helpful in teaching us about the beauty of the Creator or the creation. This is sad and ironic since so many Christian artists and musicians have historically produced such exquisite images of God and the world. Bach's St. Matthew's Passion and Michelangelo's Sistine Chapel ceiling are among countless contributions of artists in the West and elsewhere who have based their work on Christian themes. Although there is usually some correlation between what is actually happening in the world, including religious life, and what artists choose to portray, there seldom is a strong link made between art and the official theological teachings of the Christian Church.

The problem with Western Christianity's understanding of beauty has been lodged historically in the marriage of the Church's bad politics and bad cosmology, an uncreative, debilitating mix of dominant culture ideology and Platonic spirituality. Let me explain very briefly.

THE CHURCH'S POLITICS

Since the church's formal acquiescence to the Roman Empire in the fourth century, the official "mainstream" church has usually been captive to the dominant political ideology of the age. For us today, this means that advanced global capitalism, with its compulsion to generate ever more wealth, sets the context for Christian perceptions of divine life, human life, and all life, its goodness and badness, its beauty and ugliness.

It's not an exaggeration to suggest that under "Christian capitalism"—which is the dominant culture in the United States—wealth is a measure of both goodness and beauty. Christian capitalism carries an assumption that ever-increasing profit—not love or justice or compassion or creativity—is the basic motive of human labor and, moreover, that increasing ever-more profit is God's own good will, God's own good way. Christian capitalism also generates, through custom and culture, the expectation that we can, and should, possess "beautiful" things: houses, cars, land, clothing, animals, children, wives, husbands, and appearances of all sorts, including our own faces and bodies.

And yet it is also more complicated within a Christian framework. Not only has the church, under Christian capitalism, become a willing servant of the dominant political economy, some Christian groups and individuals are also some of its harshest critics. Many Christians today—politically liberal and conservative Christians, theologically evangelical and catholic Christians, in the United States and elsewhere—are concerned about the captivity of the churches to the dominant political economic system of advanced global capitalism. Although most Christians, especially in the United States, are willing consumers of capitalism, many of these same people are quick to denounce the selfishness, materialism, and superficiality of capitalist values.

THE CHURCH'S COSMOLOGY

Even more than our ethics and moral theologies, the church's dualistic cosmology has shaped our sense of what is beautiful. So while we in the twenty-first century may or may not, depending upon our politics, think of the struggles for justice and liberation as *good*, perhaps even as the work of the Spirit, we usually have more difficulty realizing deeply the struggles for justice, compassion, and peace as *beautiful*. This is because we modern and postmodern Christians tend to separate "goodness" from "beauty" and morality from aesthetics much as we do social justice from the realm of personal freedom.

Often we Christians also polarize what is ideal and what is real. Not only we do easily fail to see the sheer loveliness in all efforts to create a world of liberty and justice *for all*, we tend easily to assume that there's not much we can do on behalf of liberty and justice in this world. This dualistic perception is rooted early in the church's history, even before the books of the New Testament were completed and certainly before they were compiled and later canonized. Early Christian writers were adapting their religious experience to the philosopher Plato's understanding of what is real and what, by contrast, is ideal or beautiful. Neoplatonism, a school of Greek philosophy and cosmology popular in the early centuries of the Christian church, pushed Christian theologians' images of God, Jesus Christ, goodness, and beauty into a realm of ideal "forms" toward which human beings could aspire but never reach entirely. The things of God were, henceforth, to be imagined as "out there," beyond life in this world as we know it. Goodness and beauty were beyond our reach.

This is the backdrop to the Christian dualism that became a foundation of Christian doctrine, discipline, and worship through the work of many theologians, but especially Saint Augustine, Bishop of Hippo in northern Africa, whose teachings set the stage for much Christian thought up to the present time. From Augustine on, "beauty" and "goodness" would be ideas, more or less unreal and unrealizable in human life and elsewhere in creation. To struggle for justice, to work against poverty, to try to alleviate human or creaturely suffering would be good human work, done by Christians and others, perhaps inspired by the Spirit, but far less good than what is truly of God. Furthermore, nothing on earth, however lovely and appealing to our moral or aesthetic sensibilities, could really reflect the beauty of God which, Christians learned to believe, is beyond our capacity even to imagine. Nothing good or beautiful could show us how valuable, how good, or how beautiful God *really* is. Christian faith would teach that what we experience here on earth, at its best, can produce only intimations of what lies beyond and ahead of us in "the city of God" or "heaven."

Theologically, the Neoplatonic view of the God and the world and of what is right and what is beautiful here on earth has some moral and pastoral value. It keeps us from imagining that we ourselves, together or individually, can create a perfect world. It helps us realize, in a spirit of humility, the limits to what we can do or be, even at our best. There is wisdom and beauty in this acceptance of who we are in the universe.

But Neoplatonic Christianity has also fostered a faulty cosmology and problematic morality that continues to be damaging to God, humanity, and creation. By misleading us into believing that we are *merely* creatures who cannot do much good and whose lives, even at our best, cannot truly reveal the beauty of God, Christianity has become too often a religion of passive acquiescence to dominant political and cultural powers. Since most Christians believe we are basically sinful inhabitants of what Augustine called "the city of man [sic]," the best we can do in the spirit of the beauty and goodness of God, as long as we are in this world, is to pray for ourselves and others to be delivered from this mess—life in the world—as soon as possible; and, in the meantime, to try to do as little harm as possible. Except, from time to time, in the various liberation and reformation movements around their edges, Christian churches have fostered terribly depressive and oppressive religious traditions focused on human sin and human powerlessness to make much if any creative difference in the world.

Today in the United States, as the 2004 elections demonstrate, most Christians do not accept moral responsibility for helping build a genuinely more beautiful world for *all* of us. Shrinking in fear, most voters seemed more determined to combat gay and lesbian marriage than the ugliness of preemptive war, poverty, environmental assault, sexism, racism, and other forms of injustice being held in place by a dominant culture in which beauty leads to wealth and wealth leads to God. *Morally* speaking, the prevailing political and economic context of our life together is ugly.

Through the Eyes of Angela

Linda says that, without horses, she would not choose to live in this world, so marred by the ugliness of violence and oppression. Without the freedom to which the horses call her, Linda like many of us would be more readily sucked into captivity to the violence and sadness that seem to prevail just about everywhere so much of the time. Without the beauty into which the horses invite us to "join up," Linda and other big, strong women would have a hard time staying so alive and vibrant in a world that does its best to break the power, and blur the beauty, of both women and horses.

As it is,
Linda and I
and Gretchen the seminarian-theologian
and Beverly the photographer-theologian
have a good chortle
as we recall our sister Angela's
daily declaration to the horses
and to each of us,
*"But, **daahlings**, aren't we all*
*just **gorgeous!** "*

GRETCHEN, ARCHIE, AND PATIENCE.
FAR FROM DENOTING A PASSIVE WAITING FOR
SOMETHING TO HAPPEN, PATIENCE IS AN ABILITY TO
EXPERIENCE TIME AS A GIFT.
THE RELATIONSHIP BETWEEN HORSE AND
HUMAN SIMPLY CANNOT BE RUSHED. IT TAKES TIME.

Six *Patience*
Taking Time

Patience has been called "the discipline of compassion."[1] *Of all the virtues, it may be the most neglected, yet there is nothing more important to human, creaturely, and divine life than patience. Our impatience with ourselves, one another, and God may be the greatest stumbling block to our capacity to really experience joy and peace, as nations, cultures, and individuals.*

Movement of Time

Like humility, patience is often misconstrued as passive and weak, a signal of our powerlessness to move things along. Gretchen Grimshaw admits that, until recently, patience had always seemed to her to be "inextricably laced with an aura of subservience and inaction, weakness and wimpiness." But without patience, a person cannot ever really know a horse. As importantly, without patience, a person working with horses is in harm's way and sooner or later will get hurt—stepped on, kicked, thrown off, bitten.

Patience is not the passive acceptance of the way things are. Patience is a way of experiencing the movement of time. It's a way of experiencing time as a passage more deeply into life itself and of experiencing life more fully as an opportunity to know and love ourselves, others, and God, all in relation to one another.

Patience is a quality of spirit that horses, perhaps more than any other domesticated animal, can help us cultivate, because horses take time. As we permit them, horses take whatever time they need to do whatever they are doing—grazing, grooming each other, looking at an interesting passer-by, trotting across the pasture. When they are with us, in the care of humans, they take our time and, in so doing, slowly build mutuality with us.

Small wonder that in our over busy, over scheduled twenty-first-century Western society, so many working-, middle-, and professional class people seek ways of slowing down. Watching television, going to the movies, reading, gardening, building things, painting, throwing pots, making music, making love, walking the dog, going dancing, going fishing, playing golf, swimming, hiking, skiing, watching some sports and participating in others, hanging out in coffee shops or bars, going to the gym, going to the beach, attending religious services, praying and meditating, getting a massage, and yoga are among the ways folks in the United States today practice taking the time our bodyselves and spirits need to be healthy. Still, many people, probably most of us today, are stressed out and feel like we don't have enough time to do all that we have to do, make ends meet, honor our commitments, *and* relax.

The arrival of horses in my life—beginning with Sugar in 1999—moved me into an experience of time remarkably different than what I had known before. Although I personally had always had a fair amount of patience, I began to see, with the horses' help, what a hurried person I had become. Through my work with these animals who are spiritual mentors to me, and when I remember to set my "timer" on "slow motion" each day, one day at a time, I am slowly moving into an experience of time as an opportunity for gratitude that meets me in each moment.

Arrival of Patience

Patience arrived at Free Rein in the fall of 2000. She was loaned to us by a local summer camp trying to disperse its horses for the off-seasons. We were told that Patience was a fine teaching-horse and that kids at camp loved her. She was a twelve-year-old appendix quarter horse (a thoroughbred-quarter horse cross) who had been a camp horse since she was three.

Instantly one of Free Rein's best and most popular therapy horses, Patience was the perfect horse: able to respond to each student in whatever ways he or she needed, willing to be peppy with kids seeking a high-spirited ride, willing to plod along with riders who were a little more timid, quite willing to walk around the ring for twenty minutes but eager to jump if that's what a more advanced, independent rider wanted. In and outside the riding arena, Patience seemed happy to be with us, spending most of her time in the pasture, bonding with other horses and taking the time to just be a horse.

In the spring we had to return Patience to camp. It was hard sending her back. Not only had she become a stellar therapy horse, but also my family, especially my sister Ann and niece Isabel, had become attached to Patience. I told my friend Sandi, the riding instructor who had found Patience for Free Rein in the first place, that I would like to buy her for Free Rein if the camp ever wished to sell her. Sandi laughed and said, "You'll have to be on a list, 'cause there are folks lined up wanting to buy Patience." This was not surprising.

What was a surprise was a phone call from Sandi in the fall, saying that the camp had decided to sell Patience because she had been "running away with the kids all summer," and that the camp owner had decided to offer her first to me since Patience had evidently been so happy out at our place working with the Free Rein kids and living in a pasture.

So two days later—the day after September 11, 2001—I got myself a new horse whose name signaled a spiritual quality vital to the human-horse connection and, truth be known, to living life with any sense of perspective, humor, or serenity. Like everyone around us and throughout much of the world, Angela and I and our companions at Free Rein were reeling from the shock and horror of the events happening before our collective eyes. The arrival of a new horse, small an event as it is in the greater scheme of things, was for us a special sign of hope in the midst of the sadness and fear we shared with humankind.

Getting Patience when we did was also a good thing for our extended family because, by this time, Angela and I realized that we needed a second horse so that the two of us could ride together. Our plan was to let Patience work as a Free Rein horse several hours a week and otherwise be our horse together, Angela's and mine. We would take turns, one of us with Red, the other with Patience. As this plan unfolded, however, it became apparent that Patience was not going to work as a therapy horse, at least not at the time. She had become impatient with her routine at the school. By running out of control with students and pinning her ears back and snapping at staff, Patience made it clear that she was not going to let people she didn't know ride her or even get close to her.

Lest you think that Patience had become unreasonable, just try to imagine with me what it would be like to carry around up to an additional 20 percent of your body weight several hours a day. It would be hard enough if the weight fit neatly around your body and moved with you. Imagine, however, the extra weight leaping around on your back, poking, kicking, pulling. This is what horses often encounter in therapeutic riding and it is what they nearly always experience with beginning riders.

After ten years as a camp horse, and a year's worth of therapeutic riding, Patience was finished with this stuff. Sandi, Angela, our Free Rein colleagues, and I agreed that Patience needed one person—or, with Angela and me, two—to care for her and ride her. Even Ann and Isabel, who had come to care about Patience, agreed that their riding her was too much for the horse, at least for awhile. A horse we had all experienced as basically kind and gentle had become difficult and dangerous to her riders.

With our equestrian friends' help, Angela and I worked together with Patience and Red during the fall. We had some challenging, but often delightful, times with both horses, on the ground, in the riding ring, and on the trail. With Red, the challenge was to find ways to get her to go with us rather than pull against us. Red had no doubt, I believe, that Angela and I were her friends and that we were learning how to be in sync with her. With Patience, the challenge was to build trust—Patience's and ours—because just as the horse really didn't know us well, we didn't know her either; and both Angela and I were scared of her running away with us. She had never really done this, but she had a habit of going faster than either of us wished, so we found ourselves needing to learn how to ride Patience slowly, which was basically a matter of learning how to listen to her and how to speak to her with our whole selves.

We were planning to take Red with us back to Massachusetts for the coming winter. While we wanted to take Patience too, we couldn't afford it. To board a horse outside Boston costs roughly three times as much as in our own barn and pasture in North Carolina. As we planned our annual northward migration, we asked Liz, our friend and natural horsewoman/trainer in North Carolina, if she would take over the care of Patience for us during the winter. Angela and I both felt sad and a little guilty about leaving Patience behind just as she was getting used to us and we, to her. But we didn't see any workable alternative, and we knew Liz would take good care of her.

A week before Angela and I were scheduled to take leave of our buddies in North Carolina, Angela had the massive stroke and died. A few days later, my dog Brennan, cat Rubyfruit, and I—accompanied by Jennifer, a friend who had flown down to drive back with us—headed north for me to begin my semester at the seminary in Massachusetts. We were shipping Red north to meet us in Massachusetts, but we had to leave Patience behind.

Three weeks after Angela's death, we held her funeral in North Carolina. Beverly Hall and Gretchen Grimshaw were among our Massachusetts friends who flew south for this occasion. Patience, wearing a wreath of flowers around her neck and an empty saddle on her back, lead a procession of ashes around the pasture. A solemn drum roll, the wailing of an Australian didgeridoo, and a half-dozen horses, standing still and watching, provided the backdrop to the procession as Angela's friends and loved ones scattered her ashes over the pasture.

After the service, a couple of Free Rein's staff took me to the side to discuss their concern about Patience. She's become unruly again, they reported. She's threatening to bite people and is clearly unhappy. As we were talking, I noticed someone standing in Patience's stall. It was Gretchen who, at that moment, was stepping into Patience's life. The following is her account of this relationship.

Receiving Patience:
Gretchen's Story Told in Her Own Words

I was forty-two years old before I realized how much I had to learn about Patience. Actually, how much I had to learn from Patience about myself, and the whole wide world around me, for that matter. I think that it's safe to say that Patience has completely re-paced, and in doing so re-placed, my notion of how one lives into the fullness of time on this earth. So changed are my notions that I frequently wonder how in the world I could have galloped through so much of my own life without encountering even an inkling of the transcendent perspective that has come with my having Patience. But perhaps I can chalk it up to. . . well, maybe patience itself. Living fully cannot be rushed.

I always loved horses, although I'm not quite sure why, as I never really had any opportunity to know them, except from

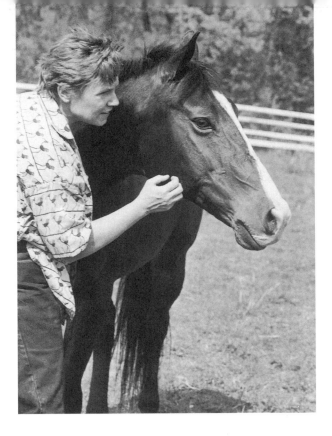

GRETCHEN AND PATIENCE.

within the nooks and crannies of my own blossoming imagination. Where I grew up, riding and tending horses was for rich kids. I was not among that lucky lot, but I spent oodles of afternoons grooming and guiding my plastic pintos and bays through the lush shag carpet that was the frontier of my bedroom corral. I read every horse story I could find from *Black Beauty* and *The Black Stallion* to *My Friend Flicka* and *Seabiscuit*. I loved to watch the powerful, majestic bodies of the wild Western herds run like the wind in the movies, although the scenes of horses suffering and dying in the movie *Shenandoah* is one of the most searing memories of my entire childhood. Growing up, imagination was pretty much the extent of my connection with horses.

Then I met Angela, Sister Angela, the Australian sculptor, nun, priest, mystic, marvelous, marvelous spirit mate about whom Carter has already told you so much, including the fact that she was a consummate horsewoman. Angela rode from the very moment that she was able sit up in the saddle until three days before she suffered a fatal stroke at the ripe, yet still rip-roaring, age of seventy-five.

At the time of her death, Angela was the subject of a book I was beginning to research and write. She was my dear, beloved friend and teacher. And Patience was among her finest offerings.

At about the time Angela took her leave of this world, Patience began to slip back into the funk Carter has described. Normally a sweet-spirited beast, she had begun to nip and snarl at the stable staff. She started to cow kick the other horses in the pasture until she could no longer be turned out with her fellow frolickers. And although she was a fine horse, she became, at that time, a poor fit for everyone except Liz, who loved her and could handle her but who had her hands full as the stable manager and as a Free Rein instructor. Patience needed more time, more undivided personal attention, than anyone at the stables in North Carolina could then provide. What to do about Patience?

This is where I stumbled, some might say rushed, to the rescue, both hers and mine. Two weeks after Angela's death, I lost my gorgeous six-year-old golden retriever, Rosie, to failed brain surgery. I was broken-hearted, and stripped down to my very socks, both spiritually and emotionally. Angela's memorial service was the following weekend and, during my visit, Carter and her sister Ann were contemplating the future of their sweet, irascible Patience.

As they discussed the matter, I heard my own suffering spirit poke its grief-stricken head out of the sand and say, quite audibly, although independently of any rational plan, that I loved Patience and I loved Angela, and I would be happy and honored to have this wonderful beast in my life. Full stop. I somewhat irrationally, yet eagerly, suggested, that I ship Patience up to Massachusetts where I lived and attended seminary, and that I could serve as her guardian of sorts until she got herself in a better spirit and perhaps me too.

Excuse me?! I could do what?! I had barely ever ridden a horse! I had no horse sense whatsoever. More importantly, I knew even less about Patience. But never mind, the Spirit seemed to know. And so all I could do was to let myself go and begin to breathe with what Angela would call joyous expectancy. I would call it pure Patience.

No problem, I thought. So I could stable her with Carter's horse, Red. I could take riding lessons with Carter's trainer, Linda. I could easily learn about fetlocks and farriers and whatever else I needed to know. I could certainly fit a saddle in the back of my sport utility vehicle. So why not? My imagination began to swell. I could spend endless afternoons in the barn and out on the trail, like in the Westerns I had loved as a kid. I could learn to jump high white fences surrounded by fields of flowers and bubbling brooks, like in the Olympics. I could wear boots and chaps and my hands would smell like leather. My internal battle of pros and cons began to kick in. It would be exciting. It would be expensive. It would be character building. It would be time consuming. It would be challenging. It would be dangerous. It would be. . . ultimately, all of those things and more. But most of all it would be, and has proven to be, among the most transformative encounters of my life, for it has been a full-on, no backing out, baptism by fire into the power of Patience.

When Patience first arrived, and my friends picked themselves up off of the floor at my news and asked the name of my new charge, I often revealed it with a flip air of it-was-not-my-choice-of-stupid-names arrogance. Sometimes I remarked, "luckily she is aptly named." Other times, when I remembered that the very luck that bestowed this majestic beast upon my humble life was linked to her erratic and headstrong demeanor, I simply said, "Her name is Patience and my killer Rottweiler goes by Happy." Either way, in her sweet spiritedness or her irascibility, Patience's name—with its modern connotations of passivity—has, from the outset, seemed to me an oxymoron to the beauty and power of her presence.

I have learned through a gentle and powerful sharing of the reins with the equine species that patience is neither for the weak nor for the faint of heart. In its etymological realm, the word patience stems from the very same Latin root as the word passion. They are cognates of the Latin verb *pati*, which is generally translated as "to suffer," albeit not in a passive way; not waiting to suffer, but actively engaging in the full offering of each moment. Both passion and patience are about diving into the fullness of time, not waiting passively for its passage. And patience, I have found, is the main ingredient in the recipe for a safe, soaring, life-giving relationship with a horse.

Patience has been teaching me that, far from denoting a passive waiting for something to happen, real patience requires an immersion in time. Like passion, patience is about an ability to experience time, to live time until it hurts, to live, as Camus said, to the point of tears.

Having Patience has helped me recast the ways in which I think about my connection to, and control over, the world around us, as well as to God. Patience has helped me revision what it means to be in control, to have authority, to exercise personal power. She has taught me to weave the vastness of time and space into the vernacular of the here and now. And occasionally, it has taken the experience of learning to share power and control, time and space, with such a worthy opponent/ partner as Patience to pry my greedy hands from the old joystick of arrogant independence by which, until the arrival of

Patience in my life, I had measured my worth.

As Carter has reflected, horses demand an inordinate amount of time. At first, this was among the greatest drawbacks of my having Patience, but it's now among its greatest blessings. The relationship between horse and human simply cannot be rushed. One has no honking choice but to slow the pace and enjoy the ride. Life with a horse requires an ongoing surrender to the exigencies of the stable situation:

The first thing each day is the greeting and sweeting of the horse, the start of the process of the daily bonding. Then there is grooming and tacking: carefully, methodically, with an air of Zen mindfulness. Then there is the ground work: slow, requiring care and observation on the parts of human and horse. Then the warm-up: gentle, controlled, conversational. The ride: focused, connected, fearless. The cool down: exhausted, appreciative, sated. The cleaning of both horse and tack: mechanical, thorough, disciplined. And all the while there is the undercurrent of pervasive prayer: present, joyous, expectant. This is what it is like to spend an afternoon with Patience. I never would have taken the time until I was taken by Patience.

It has been said that "Patience is a willingness to be influenced even when this requires giving up control and entering into unknown territory."[2] To this day this pretty much sums up my experience with Patience. She has been in my life for over a year. I have yet to sail over any high white fences surrounded by fields of flowers and flowing streams. But I don't care. And I have racked up one broken toe, one cracked hip socket, and a badly bruised and separated sacroiliac joint. But they will heal. And my hands do smell like leather, and my clothes and my car now smell like the rope-soled sandal of a French sheep herder on a hot day in August. But that has come to smell like home.

This is because Patience has added a pivotal dimension to the multifaceted social location that defines my very being. For now I am not only a white, well-off, well-educated, well-fed, blue-eyed, red-headed, Christian, lesbian, English-speaking, American, middle-aged, preacher, creature, musician, athlete, poet, reader, writer, friend, sister, lover, neighbor, theologian, peace-lugging, tree-hugging, dog-loving Libran. I am today also a horsewoman, like my dear friend Angela, and I owe it all to Patience. For it was Patience who offered me these reins and Patience who had the courage to take them with me. It was Patience who stripped me of my social status and empowered me with a sense of my own presence.

It was Patience who lovingly led me to a whole new understanding of the way God works in and through this world, and in and through me: taking the time to look and see what is really happening in the world and not simply what I want to see or what I can see easily or what appears to be. Taking time to get to know the other. Taking time to get to know myself, including my fears. Taking time to share the way rather than taking the way that would save my time, which was often simply to take control of the situation. But not with Patience. It's not the way she works and not the way I can work with her. It is also not the way God works with us.

So, with Carter, I too regard Patience and the other horses as spiritual mentors, in their own horse ways as "priests," conduits of sacred, healing power who can help mend the parts of us that have been broken, sometimes even shattered, by events and people in a world that is moving too fast for the fullness of time.

Taking Time

Dorothee Soelle, renowned political activist for justice and peace, writes of joy as changing our experience of time and bringing it into the now.[3] Like Angela, Dorothee Soelle was a mystic for whom time was an opening into an awareness of God's presence. Time, that is, when we are paying attention. "Attentiveness is a way of putting down roots in the here and now; it is an ability to exist that is practiced by a conscious and particular way of breathing and by meditation."[4]

To Gretchen and me, as they did also to Angela, horses issue a wake-up call. They insist that we pay attention; that we move slowly and patiently enough with them to notice what is going on—the wind in the trees, the snake on the path, the loud noise from the barn, the lameness in the leg, things that matter to the horse, and hence to our relationship with the horse. Horses urge us to be attentive to our own feelings of anger, sadness, happiness, expectation, fear . . . feelings that make a difference to how we relate to the horse and, thus, to how the horse relates to us. With horses, we must take the time they need and, therefore, the time we need.

Among horses' many gifts to us, one of the greatest is the necessity of our cultivating patience not simply as a way of being with horses but also as a way of being human in relation to all others, the world around us, and the Spirit in which we live and breathe and have our being. The greater our patience, the more connected we are with one another. In this sacred Spirit, once in a while the horse and rider will seem to merge: to become the same living, breathing, moving organism. For the human rider, it's an experience of sheer grace, a momentary immersion in the mystical realm of God. For the horse, we can hope that, perhaps, it is something similar, something almost as sweet as the highest quality of alfalfa hay.

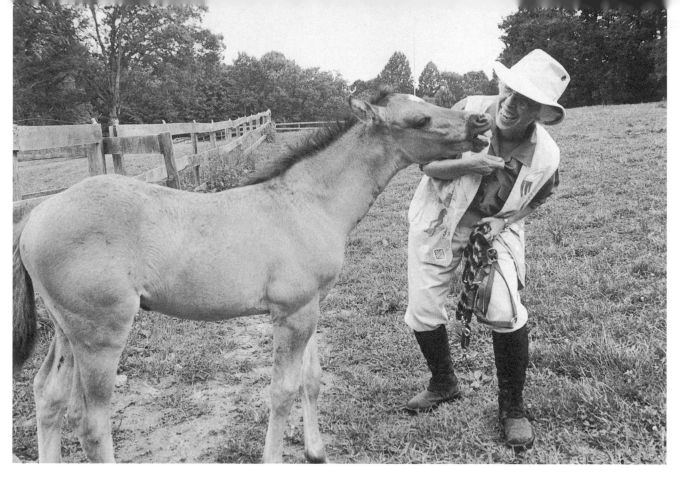

CARTER AND FEATHER.
IF I COULD START OVER, I WOULD SPEND MORE TIME, SERIOUS AND PLAYFUL TIME, WITH THE ANIMALS.

Seven *Whimsy*
Being As Light as a Feather

Against the backdrop of manmade, human-centered religion that takes itself way too seriously as God's own faith, enters the horse who introduces us to dimensions of the Spirit we may have been missing: Her playfulness, humor, serendipity, and utter joy. And we see that, naturally, God has always been here among us in this way.

Embodied Joy

In the last quarter of the twentieth century, feminism was coming alive as a force to be reckoned with inside the churches in the United States. Many women were being called by the Spirit to leave the religion that was breaking their spirits and bodies much as men have always broken horses. During this time, I wasn't alone in my dismay that women, in and out of the church, were being set against themselves, other women, and men by the strange teachings and practices of patriarchal spiritualities in a patriarchal society. I count myself fortunate that I was alive during a moment in history in which women were struggling for social and religious change through the "second wave" of the feminist movement. This second wave followed the "first wave," which took place in the late nineteenth and early twentieth centuries as (mostly white) women in England and the United States struggled for full human rights for themselves and other women.

I did not leave the church during this period because I believed that I could help transform the church from within and help call the church to work for social change. Indeed, over the past three decades, I've been able to join with many sisters and some gutsy brothers in this work of social and religious transformation. Our efforts continue as a "work in progress."

Whether or not they will have been worth it, and to whom, time will tell.

Of course, the feminist movement in western Christianity was not a new thing even in its earlier manifestations. It was kin to all those movements in history that have challenged the teachings and practices of established religion. We've been taught to call any significant departure from the doctrines, or central teachings, of a religious tradition "heresies." In fact, most heresies are rooted in intuitions of truth and wisdom that are being battered, burned, or buried by the established religion.

Like the Judaism from which it sprang, Christianity has been patriarchal to its bones. This is not to blame Judaism for Christianity's problems with women but rather simply to draw a historical line between these two major patriarchal forces. In fact, most feminists—Christians, Jews, and others—agree that, due to the strength of its Neoplatonic heritage, Christianity is especially oppressive to women. The church is certainly more hostile to sexuality than Judaism is and, in most matters, more contemptuous toward humans experiencing God in the midst of embodied pleasures, such as singing our hearts out about love and loss, marching our feet off for justice and peace, having great sex, dancing til the wee hours with complete abandon, giving birth and looking into the face of a newborn, or galloping through a field of goldenrod.

Through feminism this Christian woman has discovered that God is as fully present in the midst of our embodied pleasure, joy, and humor as she is in our suffering and sorrow; moreover, that God is as much with, and in, the earth and all creatures as she is with and in us.

Two decades ago seven Christian women coauthored a book called *God's Fierce Whimsy*[1] in which we concluded that Christian theology, in its mainstream and male-stream, has been not only sexist but too ponderous, too heavy, not reflective enough of the whimsy of God. We advocated more delightful, serendipitous, and good-humored spiritualities, all the while recognizing the terror, oppression, and suffering that breaks the world, its people and creatures. We suggested that a God who embodies the struggles for justice and peace, One whose ways are not only reproachful toward injustice and violence but also are joyful and playful among us, is, truly, a God of hope and liberation.

New Birth

I got a better understanding of "God's fierce whimsy" in the summer of 2003, when I saw her squeeze herself out into this world again, as usual wet and sticky and tired but, as usual, bearing great joy.

She was born right before midnight on June 17. Red's little filly arrived two weeks later than we'd expected. She pushed her way into this world right before my eyes and those of a dozen family and friends who had gathered at the barn to witness this birth. Two of us were present at Red's side during the delivery—Jennifer, a college student majoring in animal sciences who had been helping midwife Red through her pregnancy, and me. Everyone else stood back, outside the stall, trying to keep a respectful distance since Liz and Jennifer had told us that mares, like human moms, appreciate some space and privacy in this moment. Even Jennifer and I stood back and waited until the baby's front legs, followed by her head, began to squeeze out. Sue remarked later that the newborn looked like a "space ship" getting ready to land. At the time, Sue like the rest of us was simply awestruck. "Wow. Wow." I heard her whispering, barely audibly, again and again.

I had done everything I could to prepare for this event. But as anyone who's given birth, or even witnessed it close up, knows, there is no way to prepare fully for birth. There's something totally magical, miraculous, stunning beyond belief in that moment when new life actually appears and begins to make itself known to those who have been waiting for it to become present and to begin to take its own shape and develop its own unique personality.

Almost from the day Red came into my life, I wanted her to have a foal. I reasoned that, since she was fourteen when I got her, Red would be well into her twenties as I moved into my sixties, and I probably should be thinking not only of a younger horse if I intended to keep riding into my seventies and eighties, which I do, but also I should be thinking of a smaller horse.

On Linda's advice, I decided to breed Red to a Connemara pony, a small, sturdy Irish horse with an easy disposition. My hope was to scale down the size of Red's offspring, produce a baby with stronger legs than her mother and keep her mom's basically kind temperament.

I took great care in planning this pregnancy, beginning with being as sure as possible that Red was in good health. Our vet and others more knowledgeable than I said there was no reason why, even at age seventeen, Red couldn't have a safe delivery. Two of her previous caretakers whom I'd been able to locate did not believe Red had ever foaled, but we had no way of knowing for sure. The vet said this probably wouldn't matter provided she was in good shape, which he assured me she was.

Through the last five months of her eleven-month gestation, I was in Massachusetts teaching in the seminary. Not being able to be present with my horse during this time was hard for me, but Jennifer and the rest of the stable staff were wonderfully attentive to her and periodic vet checks confirmed that, from the beginning, Red and the little one were coming along fine.

By the due date in early June, I selected several possible names—Redwing after the mom; Ariel, after the god of wind and air; Angela or Angelo, after our beloved friend; Wingo, just for fun. But I figured that I would be able to name the baby only after the birth. Actually, I imagined the baby would name him- or herself; that I would somehow just "know" its name. I believe names are important, human names and the names we bestow upon other creatures. I knew that the baby's name, whatever it was to be, would be the right name, and that I would know it only when the baby arrived.

Like most human parents, I didn't give a whit whether the foal was a girl (filly) or boy (colt) as long as mom and baby were safe. The late arrival, which it turns out is pretty routine in the horse world, was a little unnerving, but our vet kept assuring me that all was well, and that we had done everything humans could possibly do to get ready for the imminent arrival. All we could do now was wait, and wait, and wait.

As the expected date passed and days followed days, I found that I couldn't sleep well or think about much of anything except Red and the baby. I spent most waking hours over at the stable, walking Red, grooming her, talking and singing to her, sitting on the floor of her stall—meditating, reading, thinking, praying—getting up, caressing Red's very large belly and, occasionally, feeling the baby kick or move. Red's appetite, which is always large, never abated. I was told that this was a good thing—a sign that she was feeling good and that she was eating for two.

Red may have been feeling good, but it was also a hard time for her. Besides whatever discomfort she was feeling carrying an extra sixty or seventy pounds, Red really dislikes long periods of confinement. Being a horse, like most other horses she dislikes being closed in, especially spending day after day and week after week in a stall, with only a small paddock attached for her to get out and move around in. Usually when horses have to be kept in for more than a day or two in order to recover from an injury or illness, we're able to hand-graze them, to walk them out into the grassy pastures and hold their lead ropes while they graze. A pregnant mare, however, has to be kept off the pasture because of an ingredient in fescue, a common pasture grass that can cause complications in the delivery.

In late May, once I got home from Massachusetts and then from a short, sad trip to Berlin, for a memorial service for my friend and sister theologian Dorothee Soelle who had died in April, I spent time every day hanging out with Red in her stall and small paddock. I also tried each day to take her out and walk her down the road or around the riding arena, to relieve her boredom, give her some exercise, show her some sisterly solidarity. Even though I had never experienced pregnancy myself, I felt much empathy for this horse as she waddled about in the heat of early summer, unable to play, unable to run, unable to eat her favorite grass, cut off from the rest of the herd, carrying a baby who wasn't ready, until June 17, to deliver its mom from her discomfort.

Feather

The phone rang at about 11:40 P.M. "Carter, we've got ourselves a baby coming!" the voice was pure excitement. It was Heidi, Jennifer's younger sister. They were staying over at the stables together, waiting for this moment. We had been told by some horseperson that most foals are born between 11 P.M. and midnight, and so it seemed.

Sue, Bev, and I live about five minutes from the stables, so we were able to get there in a flash, several minutes before the foal's legs began to exit from her mom's body. Red looked amazingly calm, at ease, as she lay with her head down on the fresh straw bedding that had been placed in the stall several times a day for weeks, in anticipation of this event. She was groaning but her eyes and body language conveyed no fear. In fact, whatever pain she was experiencing, I imagined, was being offset by a great embodied sense of relief.

The moment we noticed the appearance of the baby's forelegs, followed closely by its head, Jennifer and I opened the stall door and stepped in to pat and encourage Red, help the legs and head out of the amniotic sac if need be, and begin imprinting the foal, which needs to happen immediately upon a newborn's entry onto the human stage.

"Imprinting" is a process of introducing the newborn to the strange phenomenon of human life and the odd things humans do like touch horse faces, stick human fingers in horse mouths and ears and other orifices, rub human hands all over horse bodies, slap the bottoms of horse feet, and wrap human arms around horse chests and bellies. The idea is to desensitize most of the horse's body to human touch so that the horse, which is by nature a fear-based animal, will not fear human engagement.

We weren't sure whether the baby needed help getting out of the birth sac, so Jennifer and I gently cut the sac open to release the baby's face and legs. We then began rubbing our hands all over the newborn's face and legs, sticking our fingers in its mouth and ears, and massaging its wet little neck, head, and mane as they appeared. The baby's color appeared to be buckskin, light tan. As more of its slippery little body emerged, we could see that, like its mom, it had a dark dorsal stripe running down its back at its spine. Its little mane was black and looked like the hair of a punk rocker all slicked and spiked up in every direction. We continued to touch and rub everything we could.

The next thing I knew, the baby was out all the way, and Jennifer was turning it over. "We've got us a little filly!" she exclaimed.

"A little filly!" I announced to everyone. "We've got a little filly!" I echoed Jennifer and could hear the excitement in my own voice. Here she was—a healthy newborn foal, lying there still attached to her mom. We knew to leave the umbilical cord alone; Red would chew it loose when she got around to it.

One of the most remarkable sights of the evening was watching Red, having broken the cord, get to her feet and figure out how to maneuver around the stall without stepping on the one lying there beneath her. Red moved like a dancer, with grace and deliberation. She took great care to bend her body in whatever directions necessary and to lift each leg slowly, as she had to, in order to step around, over, or beyond her baby. I stepped to the side of the stall to observe for a few minutes and became aware that tears were welling in my eyes. I admired and loved this mare so much.

From that point, I have some memory of folks "oohing" and "aahing" and moving in and out of the stall for the next couple of hours as several friends helped the baby, once on her feet, try to find her mom's nipples which she seemed to imagine were up between Red's front legs.

By 3 A.M., everyone else was gone. Red was standing in the center of the stall, attending calmly to the little one, licking her all over as she lay at her feet. I was aware, as I was leaving, that I didn't know this baby's name. None of the names chosen was right. I leaned over the stall door, took one more look, thanked God for this incredible gift of an evening, a birth, an experience. I asked that she keep them through the night, and I went home to sleep.

At about 4:30 A.M., I awoke suddenly, popped up in bed, and was aware that the foal's name was Feather.

What Is Taking Us So Long?

Since that night, Feather has introduced me to God in ways that help me realize more fully than ever before that God—Holy Spirit, Sophia, she and he of many names and faith traditions and none at all—has *always* been around, through the cosmos and the struggles for justice, through our yearnings and hopes, through our sad times and happiness, through our loves and losses and gains and more losses. She has always been here with us on the earth, as ancient as the Appalachian mountains and as light and fresh as the Feather who was born in these hills, daughter of Red the quarter horse and Sebastian the Connemara pony. God has been with us in the earth's soil, with the earth's suffering and struggles for better water and air. God has been shaping and shifting the earth and other planets in and beyond the galaxies as we know them or imagine we do. The Most Holy has been with us in our most intimate relationships, in our shared sensualities and sexualities, in our celibacies and celebrations, our friendships and partnerships, our sacred unions and our connections with children and elders and one another and other creatures too. She has reveled with us playfully, leaping in joy, bucking enthusiastically, kicking up her heels when she is human and her hooves when she is horse. The Spirit has been walking us through and leading us beyond the bleakest, hardest times in our lives as communities, as individual creatures, and as the earth. She has been and will always be our power in the struggles against oppression, injustice, violence, and fear-based politics. She has been and will always be our power for right, mutual relationship; for justice, compassion, and peace. She will always be whoever she will be, and she will be our rock, our light, our wisdom, our joy, and the root of our repentance for violence, greed, and the fear in which such evil festers.

All the horses have been my priests much as they are for those who come to Free Rein and other places seeking healing in the special connection between horse and human. All the horses teach me. But more than all the rest, Feather has me by the heart and is prancing with me into God's fierce whimsy. As my Spirit-guide, she is taking me home to our jubilant Mother, wellspring of Wisdom, creative partner of the Father, lover of all creatures great and small, who surely must be wondering what is taking us so long.

CARTER AND FEATHER.

From the Authors

What Difference Does It Make

What difference does this equine spirituality make now to my understanding of Christian faith? As much as anything, the horses help me keep things in perspective. They invite me to give my religious tradition neither too large nor too small a place in how I view the world. They also suggest that I hold myself and others, horses and all creation, in a similarly measured way, with balance and patience, imagining no one of us or our "own kind" alone at the center. At the same time, the horses generate my passion. They call me to join in the struggles for justice-love, spiritual movements in which God lives and breathes, eternally generating new birth, much as she did long ago in Bethlehem, in that manger attended by cattle and sheep. Thanks to the horses, I am becoming Buddhist and Jew, Quaker and pagan, even as I am still Christian. Paradoxically, I have never been closer to Jesus. I have also never been more deeply in love with the One who takes us beyond the boundaries of what we think we know to carry us more fully into a knowledge and love of God.

—*Carter Heyward, 2005*

The Connection between Horses, Photography, and Spirituality

Horses and photography have been connected for me since I could walk.

As a young child I was propped up for family photos on a cherished hand-painted pink rocking horse with black polka dots. Then there was the "real" horse-hair horse from FAO Schwartz, the ultimate Christmas gift, though it could never come close to the live horses in Central Park that I begged to ride on special occasions when we went into the city.

Next came the annual photos taken on a beloved old pony whimsically called Mae West, who was the live prop for a roving street photographer who plied his trade on the corners of suburban Jackson Heights, Queens, where I grew up. Children would clamor to get on the aging white-faced pony with the long whiskers and enthusiastically pose for those photos that eluded a parent's camera.

Since I was taken and smitten by the "horse bug" from childhood, it followed that during my adolescent years I would devour every book written about those beautiful, daring, and engaging creatures, from *Black Beauty* to *White Mane* as well as all the Black Stallion books.

When the time came to choose a high school, I persuaded my parents to let me go away to a boarding school in the country where horses were a big part of the curriculum. "Horses, not courses" was the motto of some but I managed to excel in my studies as well as find ample time for riding.

As a good student with a passion for horses, I spent every possible moment either at the barn grooming, in the ring practicing dressage, or enjoying the freedom of being out on the trails. I not only received the coveted cup for the rider who made the most improvement, but was elected an officer of the Riding Club. You might say horses were a very large part of my teenage years.

It was during these school years that I found or rather established a link between horses and my emerging spirituality. It didn't take long before I realized that I could maximize my riding time by going to the early service at the local Episcopal Church where communion was offered regularly rather than once a month at the later family service. But in all fairness to this process of adolescent reasoning, I admit that being with horses and experiencing the beauty of the natural world with them was a profoundly spiritual experience for me. To this day, I am a devout "animal person" and, although cats have replaced horses, I need only walk into a barn to feel that I have come home.

During the process of working on this book with Carter, Angela, Gretchen, Linda, and others, I have revived my love for these magnificent creatures who, in hindsight, were some of my first spiritual teachers.

—*Beverly Hall, 2005*

About the Authors

CARTER HEYWARD is a founder of Free Rein Center for Therapeutic Riding and Education in Brevard, North Carolina. She is also an Episcopal priest, a lesbian feminist theologian of liberation, and the Howard Chandler Robbins Professor of Theology at the Episcopal Divinity School in Cambridge, Massachusetts.

BEVERLY HALL, a professional photographer living on Nantucket, Massachusetts, is well-known for her photography of children and families, often spanning generations. A 2002 graduate of the Episcopal Divinity School, she has a special interest in theology and the arts.

Both Carter and Beverly loved horses when they were children. *Flying Changes* is their first book together.

Acknowledgements

Special thanks to Pamela Johnson, Janice Brown, and Kris Firth at The Pilgrim Press for their advocacy of this project and creative work with us toward its completion. Without each of the marvelous creatures in the book—human and horse—the book would never have come to be, so we are immensely grateful to each and every friend named in these pages, especially Linda Levy and Gretchen Grimshaw. Our great thanks, of course, to our families, especially Sue, Bev, and Sascha for the constancy of their love and the inspiration of their companionship as we worked on *Flying Changes*.

Notes

Introduction

1. "Creature" and "creature-kind" refer not only to all humans and all animals but moreover to all creation, rocks, plants, stars, and water, etc.

2. Dorothee Soelle, *Creative Disobedience* (Cleveland: Pilgrim Press, 1995); originally Phantasie und Gehorsam: Ubenlegungen zu einer kunftigen Christlichen Ethik (Stuttgart: Kreuz Verlag, 1968).

3. Some of these theologians and ethicists are Joanna Macy, Thich Nhat Hahn, Sallie McFague, Rosemary Radford Ruether, Daniel Spencer, J. Michael Clark, Catharine Keller, Jace Weaver, Larry Rasmussen, Steven Charleston, Kwok Pui-lan, and Jay McDaniel.

4. In a poem written for a class assignment at the Episcopal Divinity School in the 1980s.

5. Nelle Morton, *The Journey Is Home* (Boston: Beacon, 1985).

Chapter One

1. cf. Martin Buber, *I and Thou* (New York: Scribner's, 1958).

2. cf Marvin Ellison and Sylvia Thorson-Smith, eds., *Body and Soul: Rethinking Sexuality as Justice-love* (Cleveland: Pilgrim Press, 2003), for more on "justice-love" as an undivided spiritual and ethical root.

3. cf. Sallie McFague, *The Body of God: An Ecological Theology* (Minneapolis: Fortress Press, 1993), and *Super, Natural Christians: How We Should Love Nature* (Minneapolis: Fortress Press, 1997).

Chapter Six

1. Donald P. McNeill, Douglas A. Morrison, and Henri J. Nouwen, *Compassion: A Reflection on the Christian Life* (New York: Double-day, 1993), 92.

2. Ibid., 93.

3. Dorothee Soelle, *The Silent Cry: Mysticism and Resistance* (Minneapolis: Fortress Press, 2001), especially chapt. 10, 175–87.

4. Ibid., 177.

Chapter Seven

1. The Mudflower Collective, *God's Fierce Whimsy: Christian Feminism and Theological Education* (Cleveland: Pilgrim Press, 1985).

Selected Books in Theology

Adams, Carol J. *Neither Man Nor Beast: Feminism and the Defense of Animals*. New York: Continuum, 1995.

Buber, Martin. *I and Thou*. New York: Scribner's, 1958.

Fox, Dr. Michael W. *The Boundless Circle: Caring for Creatures and Creation*. Wheaton, Ill.: Quest, 1996.

Gebara, Ivone. *Longing for Running Water*. Minneapolis: Fortress Press, 1999.

Hearne, Vicki. *Adam's Task: Calling Animals by Name*. Pleasantville, N.Y.: Akadine, 2000.

Heyward, Carter. *God in the Balance: Christian Spirituality in Times of Terror*. Cleveland: Pilgrim Press, 2002.

—————. *The Redemption of God: A Theology of Mutual Relation*. Lanham, Md.: University Press of America, 1982.

Kaza, Stephanie. *The Attentive Heart: Conversations with Trees*. New York: Fawcett Columbine, 1993.

Kidwell, Clara Sue, Homer Noley, and George E. "Tink" Tinker. *A Native American Theology*. Maryknoll, N.Y.: Orbis Books, 2002.

Linzey, Andrew. *Animal Theology*. Chicago: University of Chicago, 1995.

McDaniel, Jay B. *Of God and Pelicans: A Theology of Reverence for Life*. Louisville: Westminster John Knox, 1989.

McFague, Sallie. *Super, Natural Christians: How We Should Love Nature*. Minneapolis: Fortress Press, 1997.

Rasmussen, Larry L. *Earth Community, Earth Ethics*. Maryknoll, N.Y.: Orbis Books, 1998.

Ruether, Rosemary Radford. *Gaia and God: An Ecofeminist Theology of Earth Healing.* San Francisco: Harper Collins, 1992.

Schoen, Allen M., DVM, and Pam Proctor. *Love, Miracles, and Animal Healing.* New York: Fireside, 1995.

Sobosan, Jeffrey G. *Bless the Beasts: A Spirituality of Animal Care.* NewYork: Crossroad, 1991.

Spencer, Daniel T. *Gay and Gaia: Ethics, Ecology, and the Erotic.* Cleveland: Pilgrim Press, 1996.